BRUCE BUCKNER

D1591200

LIVING LIFE IN TERRE HAUTE

ISBN 978-0-578-20249-5

CONTENTS

FORWARD

Author Bruce Buckner is a man of his word with the distinctive drive and work ethic necessary to make any cut. It took a great deal of courage, integrity and trust to share his story without censor. The explicitly and nature of some of the elements which make up his individual journey and path he took; wasn't easy by any means.

If he continues to work hard and strengthen himself in all aspects and elevating each aspect of his life, he cannot go wrong. "This initial book has been geared to be a bestseller and is surely a page turner for all who is fortunate enough to get a copy and read it."

Hopefully this staunch literary project will be an asset to all who read it and most of all, demonstrate through the author's "real life experiences and turn-around process" how not to end up on the same path themselves.

Uchendi Nwani
Author "The Millionaire Barber"
Successful International Entrepreneur

DEDICATION

This book is dedicated to my Daughters' Brukiya, Brucoya which I love so much that words cannot express. My Hope for you two will always be that you both live a blissful life every day of your life. Make every day a learning experience Knowledge is power. One more diamond always love yourselves if you do not love yourself no one else will. Have a first class vision for yourself. When I am long gone I hope my time with you both will always empower you both to be great human beings. Be stars always show how bright you are. Brukiya Brucoya I love you two all the way to heaven. Sincerely, you're Father

"LIVING LIFE IN TERRE HAUTE" BACKSTORY SYNOPSIS

None of us come into this world with the hopes of growing up and making total messes of our lives. From the cradle to the grave a great deal of "life's minutes take place and often in no specific order. Some of our minutes are good to the cores others remain a mystery even a phenomenon. Our parents or caregivers as children play a big part in our lives. This is not to lay blame on any particular type of parenting skills or beliefs, be they good or otherwise, it's just one of many proven and relevant facts.

For a variation of reason I, Author Bruce Buckner was born in middle, Tennessee (Nashville proper) and my childhood was rocky for the most part, I came from a family of survivors and some of that survivorship didn't always stem from prouder movement. As I thank the lord for allowing me to see my early 30"s and to be given another chance to better my adult self, make my two little angels, my family and a few close worthwhile friends and mentors proud of me. The larger vision and struggle that I will eventually live and overcome is for me to be proud of.

After a youth laced with juvenile detention, the hard core streets and yes, shorter stints in state prisons, the "Living Life in Terre Haute " this brother is full to the brim of senselessness sand wasting invaluable time. Whereas the Federal prison stint in Terre Haute was by far the worse way of any human being's existence, any form of street life (or should I say street plight) is a proverbial cancer, life sucking and soul stealing way to spend your life's minutes.

I cannot take any of it back and where I've humble myself to others for the parts that I've played in each of these scenarios, I fully understand that note everyone is going to be forgiving or see it my way, which in this case, is the way it all really happen. Does this hurt or cause any form of concern to stir in me? That prior life and those awful places that you will read about in the pages to come, won't be pretty or sugar coated.

Unfortunately to survive the experiences I had no choice but to become hard, tough and still to this day have major trust issue. However, the God which I serve and continue to pray to is all forgiving and understanding. Let's clear up all a small point right here, I am not a regular Bible toting , preaching type of man and don't know if I ever will be, my goal is to just share a synopsis of my back story and hopefully prepare you for the hard cold , transparent pages of this book and the topic matters, ahead. In closing, this book will allow youth readers a never before glimpse into a world some of you may understand and fully be aware of and others of you will be shocked off your readers platforms!

All in all, the goal and purpose of the book is to share my story primarily with young men so that they not ever engage in ANY part of the sordid journey which I traveled. Of course we hope that it appeals to others and whether or not it ends up a bestseller, I guarantee you that it will be a real page turner! Thank you for allowing me some of your valuable minutes to listen to my back story and to ultimately read my book.

~ Author Bruce Buckner

I remember it like it was yesterday.... It was on a Monday morning. When a guard woke me up , "Bruce Buckner A.T.W.O.T.D all the way out the door.

So I packed all my belongings that I was taken with me. Plus the items I thought the U.S Marshal would let me bring. My mindset was on living at Federal Correctional Memphis for short FCI Memphis. For some reason I just knew the judge classified me there. Or somewhere close to my hometown which is Nashville, Tennessee

But that was actually far from the actual fact. So I ask, "Where am I going?" "Mr. Buckner we are not allowed to give you that information." "I will tell you this. You are getting on the airplane." At that very second I knew I was going someplace far away. (Based on my level of travel of travel experience at the time.)

Down at the booking area there where a few other inmates who were already in the holding cells. They were waiting for the searching process of other inmates to finish. Yes, one of those inmates was me, and a startling reality was setting in.

After being searched it was five of use leaving Mason Tennessee, for our new environment. Including me, a Mexican, a Caucasian man, another African American man, and an African American woman.

There were two white vans outside and it comprised of three in one van and myself and the Caucasian in the other van.

It took us 45 minutes before we arrive at the Memphis airport and once we arrived there was an additional waiting period before we got on the aircraft.

I could see a couple of blue planes through the fence, which was blocking the runway from the parking lot.

I couldn't see letters or markings from my vantage point or I known what carrier the plane was flying for, but I knew they was blue and huge. It was a whole hour before this small plane landed close to where we was parked . The gate open up. We drove through.

Now we were on the runway. In front of this plane that look like someone personal plane. The mason correction officers told us to exit the plane. When I stepped off the van it was freezing cold outside.

When I tell you I was ready to get on the plane, just to get warm I am dead serious!

To make the situation even worst the U.S Marshall had to search us. The Caucasian man was first I could not believe what I seen. He had to take off his shoes and socks."Damn man hurry up!" "It is cold as a motherfucker out here," Caucasian said.

All I could think is that I was next. And it is too damn cold out here to be taking my shoes off.

But there was no way around it. And my turn came in no time. But before then the U.S Marshall ask me to open my mouth, and I did. Take off your shoes and socks, he said.

Before patting my socks down and turning them inside out. Then handed them back to me.

I said to him "you do know it is freezing out here right?" His reply was, "I am only doing my job.

Then he did the regular search which assures them that I wasn't carrying any weapons or contraband. That search lasted about five minute.

However, that is a long time in the cold when you are only wearing a thin jumpsuit. When that was over I could finally board the aircraft and it was my first time on a airplane.

Once the boarding process began and I checked it all out. To the left of me was the cockpit, and I noticed all of the buttons I mean a lot of buttons, and there were two pilots seats.

The plane was full to the max.. Three U.S Marshall and four convicted felons. The two convicts that were already on the plane I could tell. This was not there first rodeo. Both were older looking.

Seem like they were in there late 40s early 50s. The big Caucasian guy was shackled up tighter then the rest of us were I could see he was dangerous. Ironically my seat was right in front of his.

It was stuff like that that made me think. Is this a sign of what type of men I am gone be around. For the next few years?

Looking out the window I saw the plane was getting filled up with gas and that was a relief.

Although this was my first time flying I was not nervous at all.

Matter of fact I was ready to see how the experience would be. When the pilots turn the engines on. All I could hear and feel were the engines roaring.

Flying for the first time was an exciting moment for me. "Hey sir I need to use the restroom." said the Bin Laden looking man. "Alright go use it then." replied the U.S Marshall. After the Bin Laden

dude was finish and re-seated I thought about taken a piss too. But when I seen how little the restroom was I decided against going.

There was way too much I had to do even with pulling my jumpsuit down .With all of the chains around my waist and the handcuff around my wrist.

Once I got back comfortable in my seat. The pilots taxied to the straightway and got in position where we could take off straight down the runway.

My heart was pumping fast too and I had that feeling when I get on a big roller coaster. We pulled off .As we were driving down the runway the plan was going faster & faster & faster.

Right before we lift off the runway I believe the airplane's speed had reach the capacity of a thousand miles an hour.

The aircraft's front went up first then the back. It was fun to me even though I was flying to another prison. All I was thinking is; way this was not a business trip or something else of that nature. I was looking out the window thinking all types of stuff. We did not know where we were going, but we were going."

Out of the blue the Bin Laden dude asks where we were going. The U.S Marshall did not tell him. This is what we all wanted to know.

He did tell us that is something he never does. His exact words were. "It is for security purposes." One of you could have people waiting at our landing location."

It just hit me. The U.S Marshall that was telling us this was African American. Look like he was in his late 20s early 30s. The reason I did not notice at first that he was African American because that is rare in the system.

There was also an Amazon Caucasian woman and I like her because she was cute. She was also thick in all the right places and she looked to be around the same age as me too. I am 28 years old at this time to give you a clearer picture.

The woman carries herself like yeah I can hang with the best of them. After taking a good look at her . It seem like she been in the army or some other branch of military service.

She had that look like. Yes I am a woman, but you all better not try me or cross any lines. Then it was this old tall Caucasian man that looked like he was very proud with his life.

I thought that in is mind he was thinking. This is my job and all I do is fly low life prisoners around to other prison. You all are scum of the Earth.

At least that is what it look like he was thinking. That is how the prison system got me reading people and I do not like it one bit.

Then again he might not be thinking that. It was probably my imagination running wild. Real testimony flying on a plane. May have been the most exciting thing I have every done. Other than seeing my little girl being born.

The plane was flying higher, higher, and higher it was so peaceful in the air. It felt like I was getting closer to God I wanted to fly higher. The sun seem like God was looking right at me. So many thoughts were running though my head. Like what state were we flying over?

Looking down at the clouds was a beautiful sight indeed. The clouds seem to look like a big sheet of ice. Being so high in the air also had me wondering how it is being an astronaut. The experience of flying was a real adrenaline rush.

The thought of my two daughters flying ran though my had too. Taking the two of them on a trip somewhere would be great adventure.

It would be great for me too. Just to see the facial expression the two might make for such an endeavor.

So I made a plan to one day for us to fly somewhere across country. It will be a Daddy Daughter Day for us.

The time came for the plane to land I am not sure .If we was in the air for hours or minutes. The airport was clear from snow, but on the side of the landing strip were huge piles of snow. The size of mini vans.

I noticing that someone had to shovel the snow off the landing strip so the planes could land. Plus snow do not fall like that.

Well I never seen any snow in Nashville like that. Getting off the plane it was a sign that read: Welcome to Indiana. Damn these people then sent me all the way up North! Those were the exact words that ran across my mind.

The judge said I was gone be close to home and obviously, that was a damn lie. The system is always throwing a curve ball. Anyway I had to accept the fact that I was gone, and be living up north for a while.

The thought of living in another state was crazy to me. In the distance I seen another white van driving to where we were sitting I knew the van was pulling up to carry us to the other prison. It did not sit right with me. This was out of my comfort zone.

My mind got to running wild again I got to thinking about my dead Granny. She been gone for 14 years now, and I still can feel her presence. As if she was a living breathing human.

People I know never laid foot on this ground. This was foreign land to me.

It was ridiculous snow on the ground back in the 90s when I was a kid. Me and my cousin used iron boards to slide down this hill in the apartments we lived in. We had snowball fight with friends , but it was never this amount of snow that I was looking at. It was so much we could have done with all of it just sitting there. My imagination was running wild.

While riding in the transportation van I was looking out the window at a lot of the restaurant that Nashville, Tennessee had. I know it was a Popeye's Chicken, Captain D's , and a Subway I remember these three restaurant because I love eating at the places. It were a lot of the same gas station we had in Tennessee on the ride to Terre Haute Federal Prison that I was taking notice of.

We had been riding for about a hour before I caught a sign which read: Terra Haute Federal Prison. Real testimony I had to piss like a racing horse.

13

It was not out of fear or anything like that because I am always ready for a fight I love my manhood my personality Getting that taking was out the picture. Yeah I got to stand all the way up in Terre Haute about mine and represent. It was a long ride down the road ahead.

The van finally pulled up to the prison gates it took a long time for the gates to open up damn! It was like the man

Was telling me to piss in the back of the van and I thought if this van do not hurry up and move. It will be piss all on the floor in the back of this motherfucking van!

That is what I said biting down on my teeth and the Caucasian was saying he had to piss now too. Wow, we both had to piss at the same damn time. It got so bad for me my bladder felt like it had fire in it, and I could not wait to put the fire out by relieving myself.

I was really thinking about making a move to that back seat area, alright finally the gate was opening up, and I did not have to. The guard proceeded onto the compound. He is still driving too "Damn Slow, said the Caucasian. " Hurry up driver I really need to take a piss!"

The guard did not give the van any gas. Even though he told him . He had to take a piss. "Man I need to use the restroom too." There was a lot of snow on the ground. Now what the fuck was he thinking? He really need to hurry up for real , for real.! We finally came to a stop. Then he decided to back the van back I thought this guard a major asshole. The door to the prison was in sight. The van stopped again, and it was finally time for us to exit the van I was closer to the door. So I jumped off first then him.

Now we were entering the doors of Terre Haute Federal Prison. Two guards put the both of us in a holding cell I walk straight to the toilet and to take a long piss. It was the longest piss I have ever took in life. That was just the first cell that we were put in. There were two more ahead.

"Buckner, Lance get your things..... move to the second to last cell." The guard said. It was no different in cell. Well I did not see a difference anyway. Fifteen to twenty minutes went by and nothing happened. Then the door opened up again. "Guys move to the last cell on the right."

We did what we was told with no questions asked. The feeling of being in a federal prison is different then being in any other state prison. Including CCA Corrections Corporation of America or a small county jail. It is some "Big Dogs" in federal prison. And I am quite sure that you have heard the stories.

Or even seen news reports about drug lords, mobsters who killed 19 people, and people that hack into computers. They have all the money in the world hidden in a stash house. Or stash houses. If not you will hear about in the coming up chapters. Now back to what was running through my head it was a lot of stories told me about prison life.

Stories like how the politics work in the federal system, etc. My mind was not on how politics was going to work, I was not gone get caught up in all that mess, just do my time and get out unscathed. But I was wondering if it were any high class famous people in this building. Because I had never been around a famous rich person before lock down.

" This really gone be some place to live Lance," I said to the Caucasian dude. The guards call us down the hallway. It was now time for us to change into our Terre Haute prison clothes. In the dress out area on the wall. There were built in shelves. In these shelves were different sizes of shoes, pants, and shirts.

The searching officer put us side by side. It was a brick wall that separated the two of use. This was the weirdest strip search I have ever done in my life! He ask for us to take off our shirt and to flip the shirt inside out, shake it out, and then give it to him. He ask for us to do the same. With our pants, socks , and, shoes.

Then he told us to stand straight up. Open our mouth "move our tongue up, down, and side to side." Raise our arms lift our feet. Turn around spread our booty cheeks open bend over then cough. Man, real testimony the last time a guard ask me to spread my cheeks I went to the hole. It happen while previously getting transferred from the state prison.

Getting in so much trouble , and even doing time on max. I really did not want to start on a bad note. So yes I did what I was told. ADVICE do what is right in society. So that you do not ever have to spread your cheeks for another man.

Plus I want these 30 months to sail by smooth as possible. After getting dress down. The guard told us to put all our old cloths in the trash can. Even the white Nikes I had on had to get thrown in the trash.

Which I was hot over because now I had to resort to wearing the blue buddies which I was giving. When all said and done. The guard walk me to an old finger printing machine. "Mr. Buckner the machine messes up at times so I will need your patience. If it does occurs" ,the guard said. " Put your right thumb on the scanner." the guard said.

As I was getting all ten fingers prints taken, and the palms of my hands scanned into the computer. The guard press enter nothing happen. Not a darn thing! So we had to go through the same procedure. Not twice ,not three , not four ,but five times before the computer accept the scans.

Finally after getting successfully finger printed, the Caucasian was next. Ironically, his prints went straight through the first time. The guard told us to take a seat in front of these two doors. One read Counselor the other door read Medical. It was about fifteen minutes. Before a man head poked out the Medical door. He ask for the Caucasian dude first. It did not take long at all for it to be my turn to see medical. He was out in no time took a seat beside me, and said "He want you now." So I walked into the office, and took a look around. He was sitting at his desk. With a computer on top of it. It was a sink behind him.

For some reason he did not look like a doctor , but more a guard. It was parts of needles on the desk top I already knew I was in this office for a TB shot. " Have you ever been Expose to TB" he ask me. " No sir I have not" I replied. " Would you like to take a TB shot today?"

" Yeah I need to know if I have been expose to it or not." He pulled out a needle, but I notice he did not have any alcohol pads on the desk. He started looking around the desk for something and it turnout was to be the alcohol pads. Just a few second he finally figure out that he had some inside the desk drawer.

Are all of them needles clean? Was my very first question. One never know if one do not ask. If you want to know something in life, ask question about the subject. There is a saying: "There is no stupid question but the ones that are not ask. " Yeah these needles are clean Mr. Buckner. The needles I have here are made for one use only, and once the needle is pull out of the person arm. The needle fall into this tube." The doctor pointed to where the needle will fall once the needle is taking out a prisoner arm.

"Alright I feel a lot better knowing that. You can give me the shot now." He picked a spot on my arm wiped the spot where I will be getting the shot. With the alcohol pad. Then he stuck the needle into my arm. " Mr. Buckner I am sure you have had a TB shot before." " Yes I have Doctor." "If a bump form on your arm. Fill out a sick call form. Because you have been expose to TB." "That is something I will do. If any bumps pop up on my arm." " Thank you for the knowledge Doctor." " Now Buckner make sure you fill out that sick call form if you see anything. Or you could just walk up to Medical. If you see anything wrong as soon as possible." After that I told him alright man I got you.

He did not have to tell me twice I am very serious about my health. I was in the office longer then the Caucasian dude was. When I walked out the office he was gone. So I took my seat back on the bench. To wait for the counselor to call me into the office. The Caucasian walk out the office five minutes later.

18

With some papers in his hand. The counselor yell out the door " Mr. Buckner come on in." The Caucasian was saying something to his self. He took a seat back on the bench, and I walked into the office and took the seat in front of the Counselor.

He did not look like a Counselor either. It was like he was role playing as a counselor. He had on a bulletproof vest. The first question that came out his mouth. " Are you affiliate with or any gang? Or have you ever been affiliated in any gang in the pass?" " No I am not sir ,no I never been in a gang before."

" Have you every testified on anyone before?" " No sir I have never testified against anyone." "If you have it is very important that you tell me the truth on this question which I am asking you." " Because you might not be safe on Terre Haute compound."

"The answers that I am giving you are the true. "Do you want to live on this compound Mr. Buckner?" "Yes sir I do I answer back. " Alright sign right there on the line." He stated while giving me a paper to sign.

After signing my name. He handed me a book. The book read Terre Haute Handbook. I got up and walked out of the office. Now it was another waiting period. We were on the bench for thirty minutes before the move was called.

My thought was this move we will be going to the units. Which is the place we would be doing our time in. "Buckner, Lance the guard called out." "Get your hand books I am taking the both of you where you will be living at for a while. It was a door that lead outside that we had to go through. Remind you, it is freezing cold outside. We had no coat. All we had on was a white t-shirt. A pair of blue thin pants, and a pair of karate shoes.

The guard said, " you two might want to run to the next door. If the door close we will be stuck out here in the cold for a while." There was a female guard 40 feet in front of us I did not see a reason to run. She would not let the door close on us. Looking back the guard was telling us this still in the door way. He was not walking with us. So I took off running to the door.(On second thought) yeah she would let the door close on two prisoners.

Entering the door. we still was not in the living area of the compound yet. The area was a hall way and one way look to be a gym. The other way the way we was walking . It was a pair of double doors to walk though. A guard push the doors open, and it was a very long walk way. This hallway stretch though the whole compound. He pointed to us the living location were we would be living . Which was to the left of us.

Walking into K-unit I took notice on how old this unit was. The paint was peeling off the walls, the floor had cracks in the concrete. And it was old broken ceiling fans. My cell number was 87 lower I walked into the cell. It was the smallest cell I have ever had to live in. The only thought that ran though my head as I was looking around. Was damn two grown man got to live like this! It was unbelievable at best. How could a man do a lot of time like this.

The people that have anything to do with Federal Correction Institution (FCI) Terre Haute should be a shame of themselves for allowing Terre Haute still be up and running.

Well any way looking around at the stuff everywhere in the cell I knew the man was a Muslim. There was a praying rug on a chair. He had onions & bell peppers in the window which I have never seen before in a cell. The windows could be open and close at will.

Now can you see the picture clearly of how old this prison is. The cell also had two big lockers which look like an old floor model television set. It was also a heater under the windows .That could be turn on & off at will. It was a shelve over the sink which was for soap ,lotion stuff like that.

My bed which was the top bunk. Did not have a mattress. So I walk out the cell. To ask the guard for my mattress.

He walk to a closet door to get me mattress. He came out with a mattress which had a sheet made onto it. The sheet was all loose hanging off and dragging on the floor. I did not complain about the mattress I just took the mattress, and walk back to my cell with it. I threw it on my bunk so that I could make my bed up. While I was making my bed up the Muslim guy walk in. He was a old man. Gray hair and everything

I forgot how the vibe was when the old guy walked in the cell, but I will tell you this. It is a big different when a man already in the cell. Then when a another man enters the cell. Just so I can put a picture in your head I want you to know my age. Around the time I was going through this hardship I was 28 years old I will be 29 in nine months.

Anyway the man that is already in the cell feels like it is more his cell then the new comer cell. He want to make you feel like every move you make. Is getting on his last nerve or in his way. Fuck that.. I always make my presence known. There are no boys in prison in my eyes. So I was not going to let nobody in Terre Haute treat me like one.

Yeah the cell is both of our property now dude. That is the vibe that I gave off when he walked in cell.

Doing time is tough I mean tough! Every man got to hold his own. Weight. If not be ready to get ran straight over. To put another picture in your head, it is gangland in there, no picnic all

Another big thing that go on in FCI Terre Haute. Is showing paper work. My paper is straight I had know worries, but I was thinking like.

If I do not know the man I am not just gone give him my paperwork without me seeing his paperwork. Real testimony it is to much information on them PSI's. It has the prisoner full name, the prisoner birthday. The prisoner Social Security number, and the prisoner address too.

For me to show my paperwork I was going to have to get to know the man. Before I set my paperwork out to him.

All I remember what the Muslim said to me he was speaking on how he was a clean person. That was cool with me because I am a clean man too, and cannot live comfortable around a messy person. To easy for stuff to get misplaced I need my belongings to be where I put them. That way I will not have to put my hands on the man around me. And the same goes for him.

He was on some USP prison stuff and he told me he like to see his celly paperwork. Then I told him "I know how politics work,. But I am gone have to get to know you. Before I set my paperwork out. Plus I am gone have to see yours too.

Real testimony I did not want to dig in all my paperwork to show another man way I am doing time in Terre Haute prison . Once I get to know you it is all good with me and do not do anything out of line and I will stay cool. After having a conversation with my new cellmate I went to use the phone. The thought of speaking to my mother came to mind. She needs to know where I am at. The way the phones where set up. A number code had to be entered prior to using the phone.

.

So I put in the one I knew from Mason Correctional Facility, but it did not work. One of the prisoners sitting in front of the flat screen television where the phones was directly in front of. Had seen that I was having trouble getting a call through. He told me I had to get with the counselor before I could use the phone.

The guy knew I was a new prisoner in k-unit I was wearing the white t-shirt. Which all new comers I got to wear. This attire had me sticking out like a albino crocodile at best! So for the mean time I took a seat to watch some television. The way the Television are set up in the Federal prisons. One needs a listening device which is a radio or mp3 player with headphones.

It was really weird sitting there watching television without sound. On top of that watching a show I have not seen in a long time. It was the Martin Show that I really like too.

The waiting process again became prevalent again. A process which I do not like doing under these circumstance. It is not fun to me waiting on something in prison. Because I am already waiting on my out date to come. So now I got to wait. For the counselor to come to work in effort to listen to the television.

Wait ,Wait ,Wait I was tired of living in prison. I knew then, when the time came for me to step out Of those prison doors, and to get back to my life. That would be the day I give the ground a kiss.

When I walked to the counselor office. It was a sign on the door that read she would not be in today. Stress really kick in on me when I finish reading that . I really needed to give my mother my location so she could put more money in my account. The only money I had was the 50 dollars in the BOP lock box. Now I had to wait 24 hours before I could do anything.

The 50 dollars could get me by for about a week. All I need to know then was when the unit which I was placed in went to commissary. A few guys at Mason put me up on .How commissary is ran in the BOP I will have to walk up to the store to get what I needed with the commissary slip filled out. I was then give my slip to the guy that was working in the store. He then grabs a shopping cart filling the cart up with the items that were on my slip. My name would be called out over an intercom. I am explaining how it was told to me. Do not think I am trying to get you ready for a Federal Prison. That is not the case at all, I want you (the reader) to see prison through my eyes.

See how tough it is because it is very tough, and not every young boy or man need to go through prison to experience it first-hand. For this is the reason I chose to write this book . To stop others from making mistakes that could land or put you in prison.

" Mainline" the guard yelled out through the unit. Everyone started taken off their headphones to place them in there chair. Guys was taking their radio to their rooms. The guys with the mp3 players put them on the charger. Then walked out the unit.

Usually I would skip the first mainline calling when I first arrive, but I chose not to since I did not have any commissary. Plus I was hungry and want to know how the food was.

Seeing the door where the guys were entering the cafeteria I noticed every prisoner who entered, had to pass through a metal detector. We also had to walk through another metal detector when walking out.

This guy in front of me ask where was I from. "Tennessee" I said. He then pointed out the Down South table to me. A good feeling ran though my body. To know exactly where my table was at because it was 50 or more tables in this cafeteria. Not to mention it would have been a pain in my legs consistently walking around looking for the table with no clue.

On the trays was chili dogs, fries ,and there was a salad bar too. More beans, ketchup, mustard, and coleslaw. The beans were looking good , plus I know that eating beans would give my body protein.

So I got me a scoop, and a scoop of mustard for my chili dogs and I took me a seat at the table. Took a bite of my chili dog. To my surprise the chili dogs was good. They tasted like they was put on a grill. They were much better tasting than the Mason Correctional Facility chili dogs.

While I was still eating my food a couple prisoners walked over to me. Everyone that have ever been lock up already knew what these prisoners wanted to know, which was where I was from. Then the question came. " Are you Bruce? "Yeah, way you ask ? "Somebody told me it was a new guy. At the Down South table. " Where you from Bruce?" " I'm from Nashville Tennessee, East Nashville Haynes Garden Apartment." "Way are you asking so many question blood?

"No problem Bruce, " I am from Nashville too, from Jo Johnson." Who else from Nashville here? Come to the gym at 6:00 P.M. "The Down South Guys will be upstairs. What is your name homie? Just call me big baby because I act like a baby sometimes." "Do you know how to play chess?" "Yeah, I am a cobra on a chess board "I said .

When 6:00P.M finally came I walked out my unit ,but did not see big baby. So I just followed the move to the gym area. To the left was a work out room. Equipped with Treadmills, pull-up bars ,and one flat screen television.

It was a room to the right that had old time prison bar for a door. In this room were 4 pool tables, but on one of the tables. A gang of prisoners was shooting dice. Trouble bound to happen with a room full of prisoners shooting dice.

So I walked up stairs where I seen 10 prisoners watching television.

On there individual 15 inch flat screen. It was also a 42 inch flat screen on the wall.

There was a room that I heard some guys in. So I walk in the room there was Big baby, Tim this guy I have done time with back home. Plus two other guys at the table playing spades. "What is up Bruce when did you get back lock down?" Tim ask me. "Three in a half years ago."

To my surprise I at less knew one person from home. "Who else up here from the city?" These two guys here. It is one more guy from the city, but he really does not come out the unit. " Way you were not at the Down South table?" I ask Tim the prisoner I knew from the city. "If you do not no Bruce I am a Muslim now." Tim said.

The first thought which came to my mind .Way does a man come to prison than turn into a Muslim. Knowing damn well he knew Christ Jesus first. It have been a few times I have meet a man that knew the Holy Bible first, before becoming a Muslim.

Then find his self in prison then change to another book. The way I look at it the man that switch to another belief. Was deceive by another man. Which make him a weak minded man.

For the record I have nothing against other religions practices if that was what your parents taught you to believe as a child, then stick with that. Parents want the best for their child, not a man you met while in prison which he has only known for a couple years.

I believe if he did care. He what have asked what religion did you grow up believing? Then advised you to put your time and energy in that specific religion.

Not deceive you to switch over to theirs that just do not sit right with me, but that was on him not me so I just let it go.

The gym area close at 9:00P.M so around 8:58P.M the move was called. Lock down was at 9:30P.M so I took a seat in front of the television until it was lock down time.

The first night in a new place is always strange I did not want to live like this. Both of us do not know how the other one does his time.

It just not a good feeling being in prison I was at the top bunk which I do not like at all. Because I use the toilet a lot at night. Using the toilet kept me one step ahead of my cellie. He sleep I am not get the picture.

Even though it is weird being the new man in the cell I make myself at homes fast.

The feeling did not stay with me long and on the muscle I told him "I will not be cleaning up after him, I will not put up with stealing!" " I am man that demand respect. If I got a problem I will handle my problem as a man." I made eye contact with the Muslim and If he did not like what I said it what have been a fight that night.

After I said what was on my chest I Jump back on my bunk.

That first night was a long night. The damn man kept me up all night snoring.

All I was thinking is "this gone be a long two in a half years Bruce." It was finally morning I got up wash my face, used the soap, toothpaste, and Degree deodorant I was given from a manin the Down South car until store day. He also gave me a pair of new shower shoes.

The guy name was Al, from Kentucky. He was a real cool dude. Well any way after I got myself together I went too watch some television. The stair I was sitting in (I just knew) it was somebody seat. No one stepped up to say something to me about where I was sitting so I stayed seated until breakfast was called. On this morning day pancakes was on the line. The pancakes that Terre Haute serve are real . Not that out of the box stuff.

When I got finish eating my breakfast I went to laundry. For my cloths exchange. The line was out the door.

It was guys with boots in there hand others with sheets and blankets. It was another group of guys who were just walking in. The line was at a stand still I made a decision to follow the group. It was a good decision because the line for cloths exchange. Was not as long , but it was still a crowd I looked around to see if the Caucasian. Was somewhere in the laundry room. He was over on the far end of the bench just chilling waiting for his name to be call.

One look at him you would not know that he had been in the Federal Prison system for 10 long years. He definitely was not a rookie doing time. The rules with politics what to say how to say it. Who not to speak to, and who not to look at too long. Being in prison 10 years is a long time.

It took around thirty to forty five minutes. For the workers to put me in the system and to give me my clothing. Getting the right sizes from them would be a blessing . Either the pants was too small. Or I did not have all my socks in the bag. The workers be moving too fast with all the energy and testosterone in prison. Really not caring if he is giving the other prisoner the correct clothing. Be miss placing some items.

So before I step out the door I check my bag thoroughly. If I was to leave the area and then found out something was missing in my bag, it would have been fruitless.

The guard would have not let the workers correct the mistake and give me the things that I was not giving.

The clothing item at Terre Haute which I most appreciate was the thick blue coat with the orange hat. Back at Mason Correctional Facility the coats they give are thin. The cold air cut through those coats like a razor blade.

While exercising on the yard with the big blue coat I could exercising and stay warm.

Back in my room I decided to clean out my locker. To neatly stack all my cloths in the small area of the locker. Inside the locker which a bigger then most locker spaces. It had shelves inside to separate different areas of the locker.

After putting my stuff up I walk over to J-unit. Because my counselor was not in the unit. I really needed to get my phone account set up and to call my mother to tell her where my location was. The door was open.

A prisoner was talking to him. A few seconds of me waiting at the door the prisoner walked out. "Come on in." The counselor said, I walked on in and took the seat in front of him. Once I made eye contact like a man. " My name is Bruce

Buckner I came in yesterday. He logged into his computer. All I could think was a computer is a very powerful tool.

That stuff he could be looking at about me could be wrong. Then he hit me with what he just got finish reading which was not at all correct .

The counselor said to me that I owe court cost. Which had been paid when I was in the federal holding facility in Bowling Green Kentucky. "That must be a mistake" I said. "That was paid off in 2011.

"Mr. Buckner it was not paid off I will do this for you. Tomorrow I will check with the court. Now what is your judge name?" I replied Ms. Trouser, or something like that because I had forgotten her name.

"Do not worry about it, just be back in my office tomorrow." He printed off some papers than handed them to me. "What about my phone call pin?" Your pin is on one of them papers I just handed you.

Mr. Buckner make sure you be back in here tomorrow. If the court cost was not paid. You will have to pay.

Pay it all at once? "No I will put you on a contract and the contract will read that you Bruce Buckner will give Terre Haute permission to take twenty five dollars off your account every three months. If one payment is miss. The money will be taking off every month. Also if you miss a second payment you will not be able to buy from the store until the courts are paid off in full.

The payments will start in June. "Okay that was cool with me." It was February that date we discussed was a whole four months away. That was plenty of time for me to stack up on commissary before I start paying.

"Mr. Buckner just so you know the money will be taking off every first of the month."

Every first of the month I will make sure at least twenty five dollars is in my account.

"Anything else Mr. Buckner?" My answer was no.

I walked out the office reading over the papers the counselor had just gave me. It was two numbers I had to remember. One was my phone pin. The other was my computer pin.

Back in the unit the computers were full plus it was a lot of guys waiting around to jump on one. "Who last on the computer I asked? This dude that I was beside raised his hand " I am." Two guys got up at the same time and me and the guy beside jumped on those computers.

The computer got a device on the right side where a finger print is read. I punched in may pin number. then push may finger print down and the computer screen showed eight different headings. Music Terre Haute, bullet board, and account transaction. The account transaction is the heading I click. My account had more than I thought. It was a buck sixty ($160.00). Last time I check my mother put fifty on my account. She really been the only person with me on this bid I was ready to go to the store with this hundred sixty dollars

Today was Tuesday store day for k-unit and everybody was talking about some new ice cream the store had gotten in stock. I ask the guard for a commissary form. Now I was really ready to see. What type of items the store stock.

The form had Nikes, Adidas, and New Balance. Some shoes was gone be my first purchase, plus a radio. Just those two items was a hundred plus.

Some dude up stairs was hanging over the rail. With some Adidas in his hand for sale. The same ones that I wanted. So I holler at him about the shoes. "Bring the shoes to my cell So I can check them out. He came down to my cell which was 87 lower.

The first thing he said was " I only put them on twice. To take some pictures.

You can see the shoes are still new." I took the shoes out of his hand and the new smell was still there. The bottom were still new looking . "How much you want for the shoes" I asked?" "Thirty five dollars."

"Yeah I want these." Are you going to the store today? " Yeah I am." Okay I am going up to my cell to fill my list out." "Before you leave what time do I need to be at the store?" "You can go after lunch or after dinner." He walked out my cell.

After giving me the information I needed. Ten minutes later he came back to my cell. With a list of the items he wanted me to buy for the shoes. I took the list with the form. Did some adding to make sure the list of items add up to just thirty five dollars, and not a penny more, because prisoners always trying to scheme!

The list was proper. So filled out my commissary sheet. Coming out the cafeteria the store location is to the right. That was my destination. When I walk through the door my first thought was damn the whole room was full!

It was really like a real store in the free World, and was run the way the stores are ran in the free world. For example when stores are open late night, and there are bulletproof window between the store clerk and the customer for protection. When you pay the clerk place your item or items through a metal box. That is exactly how the store is in Terre Haute.

Some of the prisoners that came in late were jumping in front of the line. Paying the workers stamps to get there items to the cash register. I saw at that moment the store workers were hustling. Nothing wrong with a side hustle. Plus the hustle never stop I thought, but I was not gone pay for that service. I was not in a rush to leave.

It was a whole hour before I got my commissary items and was out the door. Back in the unit in my cell I separated the items for the shoes. I put my shoes up against the wall under the bed. To wear after taking a shower.

Put the items in the laundry bag, walked out my cell handed the prisoner I bought the shoes from the bag. Now I had food to eat, some comfortable shoes to wear.

My next goal was to find someone with a radio for sale and that did not take long. This dope smoking looking prisoner had one for sale. As bad as I wanted to watch Martin I bought the radio for fifteen dollars. It was one of them black radios which took two batteries. On the real I should have bought me a Mp3 player first.

By me having a Mp3 player I would not worry about my batteries going dead or having to purchase a pack of batteries every week. Then it happened, my fear was confirmed the radio sound was getting low. The cheap ass radio I bought from the other prisoner was a tank.

What I mean by tank. The radio drains the batteries to fast. Not even a whole week went pass I needed some more batteries. At that moment when the sound got low on my radio I knew I had to buy an Mp3 player, and get rid of this dud product I had in my possession.

Some new prisoner was assign to K-unit and that was my chance to put the radio up for sale.

My price was eighteen dollars for the radio. It was a small profit, but that was alright with me. It was a Tuesday morning. The day I been waiting for. Today I would buy me an Mp3 player. The reason that Tuesday's are so special is that on Tuesday, the store has open house. Tuesday is the only time the store sale Mp3 players. Plus other stuff we are not allowed to buy on a regular commissary day.

Lunch was called, but I did not eat I went straight to open house. To my surprise it was not pack either.

It was so empty that I walked straight up to the window. "Give me an Mp3 player. One Mp3 cover too." "We have a Mp3 player for you to purchase, but no Mp3 players covers in stock right now Buckner. Come back next week. The store will be stock with some by then."

That is what the lady behind the glass told me. By her telling me to come back next week, she irritated me. Another reason to stay away from crime so you want have to experience. The way it feels to become impatient.

It is not a good feeling waiting on something in prison. It is much better dealing with something in the free world. So if you are in a rush to get some money the wrong way, stop what you are doing right now!

It is not worth being in prison for. Have patient at home with your Mother or whatever it may be because you might find yourself in prison. Getting irritated over something as small as an Mp3 player cover is not good for your health. So again practice patient at home.

After all was said and done, I came back to my regular self and calmed senses. I took the Mp3 player walk back to my unit. Got me a seat and pulled out the instructions to read over them. The problem of buying batteries was no longer a factor.

There was an Mp3 player charger connection on the wall which could charge twenty Mp3 players at once. Now it was time for me to go outside to lift some weights. The Down South Car exercise at 1:00P.M Monday-Saturday. No matter what the weather was at the time.

Every day we work a different muscle such as Mondays we work our back muscles, Tuesday (which was the day in question) was bench press. Tuesday was my favorite day of the week while Living Life in Terre Haute. Wednesdays is arm day I liked arm muscle day too. Thursdays we work shoulder muscles. Thursday was an enjoyable day too but Fridays was my least favorite exercise day. Real testimony I hate working my legs. When I am in the bed after a tough day of working legs I am in too much pain.

After working legs I am in need for a rest day. So I skipped Saturdays sometimes. Soon as the next exercising day came the whole Down South Car would jump on me.

Mad because I did not show up and that would piss me off too! It seem like everybody was trying me. Acting like they my daddy and that is a serious problem being lock down in prison. Strangers want to act like a man parents. That is a key reason way I could not wait to get out of prison.

A man mind is all the way off track and being off track so long, it would make you forget who you are. It is so much negative thoughts and actions that go on in Terre Haute Prison or any other prison.

The down talking to and on each other, playing and reckless eyeballing is normal, but you were not raised to tolerate such things. This is how it work being lock down. You either go hard or take a lot of disrespect and go home. If your choice is to go hard be ready to lose out dates.

Being locked in a cell 23 hours a day for 24 hours on the weekend. It is nothing nice being lock in a cell for a long period of time with another man that you know nothing about. For example, he might be a big time serial killer. One more example, he might be something worst like a man rapist. A man that you really did not know exist but they do. So ask yourself before you commit a crime. Am I ready to live with a man that likes me sexually?

Choice two you take all the disrespectful stuff. That comes your way without putting your hands on that man. It will really be tough going that route because anything goes in prison. Prisoners do things you think they should not do because you know the true meaning of respect. If you can put up with the disrespectful things you go home.

Choices are important so please read and learn from the words in this book. Change your ways for the better and never have to experience the way man live in prison.

Well at the time I wrote this book. It was my second time doing a bid. The first time the judge gave me a year day for day. This was a slap on the wrist. By that being my first time doing time I felt like I had something to prove. So I got into fights with all type of guys. Even catching a extra charge. The one year turned into two years and one month.

On the second bid I wanted it to roll by smooth. It has not, I do not know if I have talked to you about what I am about to tell you.

Before I came to the federal system my residence was West Tennessee State Penitentiary. It was the initial part of the Terre Haute bid

I was finishing/flattening a 8 year sentence which I thought I would be going home once it was over. On top of that I was thinking my federal time was encompassed in that bid. Or that it ran in with my state time. Not the case at all. The day I thought I was getting out and going home, the U.S Marshals was at the entrance.

*Note: So I am advising you with all my heart. Take my experiences and learn from them. Please be serious with your life direction after reading this book. It is meant to show you paths which not to go down and mistakes not to make.

Stay away from negative places and stay away from negative people. If not, you will only fall into a vicious way of living. Not really living, existing actually.

It will be hard because the vicious people you encounter just keep on biting and stabbing you in the back. Do not end up in prison because you will meet your match. You probable thinking you can fight huh?

I mean you gone run into somebody older, bigger, and much stronger than you that can really fight.

Put yourself around positive places with positive people so you won't have to experience this kind of stuff.

If you do end up in this spot, it might be hard to break away from it. All I am saying break away from the vicious life while you are free. God put us on earth to be free, not living in a place where it is hard to breath. It is quite claustrophobic in prison.

Being in prison is hard on top of it being hard a prisoner who has kids (which I do) means that all of the time that a man miss out of his kids' life. Well, it hurts a man a lot. There is stuff inside a real man that he want to teach his kids.

Being in prison the man cannot guide his kids in the way they should go and that really is painful beyond words.

One Saturday I had a visit from my mother and she had my daughter with her. I had not seen her in three years. When I left home my daughter was 5 years old. Now she was so much bigger. And she was talking more.

Plus on top of her getting bigger her 9th birthday was in 4 months. She was the smartest girl I had every talked too.

She ask me when was I getting out? The kind of daddy I am I told her the truth. At that my answer was in two more years. She said, "That is to long daddy I will give you to next week."

That almost brought tears to my eyes; she really wanted me to be home but I could not give her what she wanted at the time.

After the visit I went back to my cell and climbed on top of my bunk and just thought about how long 2 years is to a child.

Being that young waiting on different Holidays such as Thanksgiving, Christmas and waiting for the summer to come around. That is a long wait to a child. Please just think! Would you want to take your child though a bid with you?

Now really think hard before you make a decision. Be careful with your life, have a productive and a sincere purpose.

On August 29, 2014 I went outside on a free day. The only reason I made a decision to go outside on this day is because I woke up on the right side of the bed.. It seem like the whole compound woke up on the right side this day.

My morning went by pretty good. So I thought about walking around the track for a few hours. Fellow prisoners that I never talk to were walking up to me making conversation.

That was weird because guys in prison always have some type of (underhanded) motive. It is hard for me to see the truth in the words some prisoners speak. That is something that I do not like a human that lie. Some are con artist always trying to con the next man. Trickster always wants to break the rules and get away with something.

To sum it all up for you Prisoners are very cutthroat, so I really do not talk much. Nor do I want to meet new frenemies (friendly enemies). My friendship always ends up in a physical fight.

Some of my previous turned into a enemy I learned from that and that is way I learned to stay to myself.

It is no way to be friendly in Terra Haute or any prison in America. Those relationships usually end up turning sour. Every man will try to out man the other. In Terre Haute Federal Prison every man want to be a boss or under boss, because he was one in the streets.

Prison is not the streets, its way different. Thinking otherwise generally leads to grave misunderstandings.

One time this particular prisoner sat beside me in the television room and began talking to me about what he had on the streets. What states he went to just to shop. Now me being the man I am. I wanted to know what he did to get to that level because I been in the game along time.

Having that kind of money he was talking about having would have brought forth a whole lot of problems. He told me one day it was 50 pounds of purple. Which is marijuana in the trunk of his car in his garage. "Bruce that was something small I was getting 2500 pounds when my Mexican Cartel man was pumping." His cousin broke in his house looking for the stash and not knowing his mother was there. The cousin grabbed his mother shot her nine times. All because she did not know where the weed was hidden. Man, after hearing that story I knew I was never selling drugs ever again!

He ask me. "What will you do if somebody shot your mother?" My answer was I will hunt them down then kill him-whoever it was.

Then I told him a story about when I was buying a brick in the streets. "Homie I use to front this dude the drugs and on top of that I had a spot where I would let my workers sit in to get the drugs off, and the spot was doing numbers too. One of the workers I was fronting the drugs to broke in my house."

This dude identity is anonymous and I have to keep it that way. He younger than me, but he was one of the real bosses. He showed me pictures with him and rappers "2Chainz" & "Juelz Santana" in the studio. He and I never fallen out. He was one of the few that were really real. He left the unit shortly after we got to know each other.

He had signed up for the drug program in L-unit, which was located right next door.

Back in my unit I got my stuff to take a shower. That is my routine when I come back in from outside.

After my shower I cooked myself something to eat. My meals consisted of Salmon, Tuna, Mackerel fish which all give my body the protein it need to grow muscle. Sometimes I'd eat me two bagel sandwiches with potato chips. On the sandwiches I spread jalapeno cheese on both sides of the bagel .Then I cut the big salami sausage in eight big slices.

Once I figure out which slices best fit together I'd arrange the salami slices in four pieces on each bagel. Then I put jalapeno peppers on top of the meat; pop the sandwiches in the microwave for 2 minutes. Once the bagels were done I'd walk back to my room to grab a bag of BBQ Corn chips in my locker. I'd top the meal off with a blue cool aid pack.

After grabbing my cool aid pack I walk in the TV room. At the time it was only a few guys in the TV room, watching a show I did not like. "The Bad Girls Club". The rerun from last night I could not enjoy eating my food watching this show.

So I ask "is anyone of you watching this channel?" "No go ahead and put on something else" I place my food in the chair then change the channel to something I liked watching. Which was BET (Black Entertainment Television) A good movie was on? The movie "Love" if I am not mistaken. The movie where actor "Common" is in teaching his nephew or cousin how to be a man.

I set back down in my chair and Grabbed one of my bagel sandwiches out the bowl and took a bit. Then grab a hand full of BBQ Corn chips. The taste was great I enjoyed every bite.

A thought came back to mind… Today was a good day even in prison but I knew something was not right about that feeling.

I"Damn do I suppose to be feeling like this?" I ask myself. Prison was confusing me. At that point in the TV room I knew that a change had to be made in my life. Flashes of my youth was coming to mind. The way I was raised I knew better then what I was showing.

I should have made better decision, picked the environment that I was hanging in more carefully. I should have picked better friends to hang with. Surely, prison life was not meant for me.

It was the streets that put me here; I was out there chasing a life not accustom to me. So if you are reading this book. "Please, Think, Think, Think, and Think hard about where you want to be in your life. Where you really wish to be in your future ahead. What (legal and moral) path and career is going to take care of you? I cannot stress this enough and understand that I speak form hard won, experience

Please make right decision in your career and of all things, do not become a career criminal. Becoming a career criminal is not worth it, nor is all the time you will spend in jail or prison.

Getting a job at a place that you do not like is even better. The reason way it is better is because you may not like the workplace choice (at the time), but you will be getting paid. Not to mention that you won't have to look over your shoulder and you get to go home and have a respectable income coming in.

Look at it like this you could be shift supervisor or even a manager in a few years by working hard. But as an inmate in prison you will not like the place, have no income coming in and you cannot go home.

Prison is an awful place where people rot. You become scum of the Earth and being in prison is the next thing to being dead in a grave.

After eating I walked back to my cell to wash my bowl and cup out. This way no bugs will smell the left over crumbs in the bowl and then decide to raid the room. The prison is over 70 years old I did not want to welcome any spiders, ants, roaches or any other creepy crawlers into my area.

A couple of months passed I was getting feed up with my cellmate it was time to make a move and fast. I could not put up with the snoring anymore! Then on top of that he was one of those prisoners that like to get the cell painted.

That paint smell is too strong to be around I found a cell that I could move into.

It was the next day when I made the move. Three cells to the right. My new cellmate did not like the bottom bunk and that was a plus for me. It had been a while since I had the bottom bunk so this move was good.

We made small talk while I was putting my property up. He ask me where I was from? Nashville Tennessee was my answer. Then he wanted to know if I knew the same guys he knew, from Nashville. That he was lock up with at a different place. Some of the names he mentioned to me I did know those guys.

After he finish asking me question he then told me about himself. The first thing he told me was that he was a Vice lord. The reason being he wanted me to know people had his back, but I did not care about that. If it ever came down to fighting we would be two men fighting alone against each other and I was gone make sure of that.

The next morning I decided to go outside for an early workout. The muscle I was aiming for this morning was back. When I walked up to the machine it was no weight on the bar.

Getting warmed up is very important I put one 50 pound plate on the bar for warm up. I got into stands so the weight lifting will be comfortable the reason being I did not want to injure myself. First I started off with 10 long reps 10 short reps then I put another plate on the machine, and did 10 short reps 10 long reps again.

Now I was warmed up my next plate was 75 pounds. All of the combined weight together was 175 pounds. I did 20 reps long 20 reps short, and my last plate was 75 which brought the max weight to 250 pounds I did the same amount reps for that set too.

My next move was to walk around the big track for a minute. Walking around the track is a way that I gave my body a little rest. Plus it gave me time to think too. There were not a lot of prisoners walking around the track I had most of the track to myself.

After my body got some rest I got on the pull up bar. Having a good pull up game was a goal of mine. The way I do my pull ups range from 3 different types of forms? My first set I do is hands close to each other inside of my hands facing me doing10 reps of them. Still strong I jump off the bar then I go right to doing 10 burpees. Get back on the bar place my hands a little farther apart inside of my hands facing me doing10 reps again,

The last set is a little harder than the first two sets. So I do just 9 reps but I jump down and do 25 burpees. Just to make up from missing a rep. All together I do ten sets. Add it up a lot of work, but I liked it.

It was almost time to go so I walk to the exit gate. It was a crowd around the exit gate. Some prisoners sitting down chilling looking like a power, move not scared at all. I was at a table waiting for the gate to be open, plus not scared either. Some in groups looking scared of Terre Haute to me.

The move was called over the intercom. The crowd poured into the gate .It was yet another door that had to be open before we were able to enter into the building. For some reason it was another 10 minute wait before the door was actually open.

The next thing I had to do was take a shower. That was every prisoner in Terre Haute routine every time coming back from outside it was shower time. It was only 4 showers in the unit so the best thing was to always have your stuff ready when you walked in your cell. That is what I always did; I was either first in the shower or next in the shower.

The next for months my cellmate will be going to the Half-way house. That was all he talks to me about. What he was gone do when he get out I was no hater.

It fact I was ready for him to go anyway. He smell like shit to me sometimes and plus he was a grimmer type of celly, but he did not get in any trouble. When he was finish talking to me about his release date, I would say "I am ready for you to get the hell out the cell too, and up out of my face.

The next day the unit was flooded with guards and all the cell doors was open. Every prisoner was asked to walk to the gym. Everyone seems confused like what was going on. My first thought was a massive search. We were all in the gym talking and waiting. Some guys were nervous because it was either cigarettes or a remote to the television in their cell. Both of the items are contraband.

No one wanted to go to the SHU (the hole) for contraband- or any reason. It was an hour in a half when the guards walk back into the gym. We had to get in a single file line. The guards search the area we were all sitting in. Then search us before allowing us to walk back to our cells.

The vice lord was the first one in the cell. When I walked in he was already in the cell for a few minutes. My stuff was everywhere. Even the stuff that was in my locker was scattered all over the cell. "Something was not right how did my locker get open?" "Bruce on the back of the combination lock a key goes there." The vice lord told. That was when I found out the guards can get into the lockers without the combination.

Getting all my stuff together I notice my Polo cologne was missing. "Where my Polo cologne at?" I ask him. "Shit I do not know." he said. That was not good on any level. I hate when human beings still from me. Or evening think a human stole from me. Before I did something that would put me in the SHU I went to ask the first person I saw.

"Do the guards take cologne?" No he said. After hearing that I knew the vice lord prisoner had my stuff. He tried to say he did not have anything to do with the cologne being missing. It was getting serious my blood was boiling he knew I was gone do something to him. When it was all said and done he bought me a new bottle that following week.

That got me a little stress because I told myself that no matter what I was not gone fight at this prison. It was a close call for me. By me being stress about what type of men I was around I made a bad decision by smoking some weed. Smoking weed in prison took me to a whole other level. Man when I walked out of my cell high I wanted to fight everybody. Every prisoner I had a problem with in the past I walked up on to see if he wanted to fight.

After checking every prisoner / cell in the unit I walked over to M-unit. Real testimony I was on some start a war with other cars. The reason I walk over to M-unit was to check on big baby. See if he was alright if he had any problems with anybody because we were going to take care of it on this day. My next move was J-unit.

It was a prisoner name Shayne in the Down South car in this unit I did the same thing in j-unit. But I got out of hand and too loud I was asking did anybody have a problem with the Down South car. Say something we can handle it right now. Nothing was said. Finally the guards came and got me. "What is wrong Buckner?" Nothing came out my mouth not one word was said.

All I did was turn around so he could put the handcuff on me. All I could think was damn, I am going to the SHU!

The first place the guard walk me to was the lieutenant's office. He gave me a chair to sit in. "What is wrong with you Buckner?" "Just having fun sir that is all." "Do you know what you was doing was wrong?" "What are you talking about I did not do nothing wrong." "Buckner you were walking around the units trying to fight other prisoners." At this moment a nurse came in to take my vital signs.

It was strange too me I was wondering do these people know I am high.

The questions were over I was just sitting in the chair waiting for a guard to come get me and walk me to the SHU. The guard did not come get me to walk me to the lock down unit.

They came to walk me to a white van. It felt like I was getting released, but I was not.

Inside the van I could not stay still I wanting to see everything out both windows. One minute I was looking out the right side window. The next minute I was on the left side of the van looking out that window.

It was a whole, entire 25 minutes before I reach my destination. The van pulled up at a hospital. My hands were still handcuff behind my back. The nurses grabbed me by my arms and walk me to a bed. One guard ask me to turn around so he could take the handcuffs off. Then he tricks me by cuffing one cuff to the bed. At this time I was thinking how I got myself into this.

It did not sit right with me. The nurse came back in. With a cotton robe for me to put on. The one that have a patient's ass hanging all out I kept my boxers on. Before I could walk out the restroom. A guard reach in the door to give me a cup to piss in I walk back over to the toilet to give the guard a piss sample I was for sure it was gone come back dirty.

Then after I got back in the bad to watch television Deadliest Catch was on. It was a show I liked to watch when I was home. Just by watching the show made me think about moving up to where the Bering Sea was located to apply for the green horn position. Being a felony that should be a job I can get with no problem.

By me being the new green horn the crew will be super hard on me, but I will be able to handle the position. Plus I will be able to eat all the sea food I want.

Two nurses came to get me for another move. Both nurses were holding me by my biceps. The one on my right said "what big muscle you've got" I felt like Hercules after she told me that. The two nurses walked me to an open pace area. It was about 20 beds in the area I recall five other prisoners hand cuff to the bed.

I was trying to see if I knew any of them or any of them knew me. No one had on prison cloths I could not tell if the prisoners were from a jail or from a prison. The nurses help me get into my bed then walked off I was handcuffed again.

It was embarrassing to me all I could think of was covering up my face. So I pulled the blanket over my face and went to sleep. About an hour went by a nurse came back. To give me a shot in my arm. "What is going on", I asked. "We think you were going through a Schizophrenia episode."

After hearing that I went back to sleep. When I woke up it was breakfast time I was served cereal, blue berry muffin, and a banana. She also gave me a cup of orange juice plus milk for my cereal.

It was hard for me to eat because I was handcuff to the bed. It was even more embarrassing I was a grown man feeling like a baby. That is way you should never want to experience being in prison. Prison pulls a human being out of touch with one spiritual self.

After breakfast I went back to sleep with the cover pulled over my head. Now it was around noon because I was woke up by the nurse with a tray beside me. For lunch I ate beef burrito with sour cream, corn, and potato salad. With fruit punch cool aid to drink. The food was so fresh to me. In reality I knew this was not gone last long.

With that in mind I went right back to sleep. It was sleep that I really needed. No worries of killers running in my cell I could sleep as long as I want. That felt good to my soul. The hospital was nothing like Terre Haute units with prisoners walking up and down the range. Sitting close to your door playing and gambling which cause each prisoner to eventually talk loud.

Do not get it wrong I was still embarrassed. Just a little more relaxed and that was peaceful.

My food was being brought to me by a woman. Consider the reality of my living environment in Terre Haute Federal Prison I could do the rest of my time in this hospital bed. Around 6; 00 P.M dinner was brought to my bed side. This tray was the best spaghetti, Caesar Salad, a fruit bowl, and last but not least garlic bread with sweet tea with a pinch of lemon flavor to top it off

This time after eating I did not go back to sleep, but watch some television. Dual Survival was on. It was a show about surviving in different environment and in extremely tough circumstance. It was like the hospital trip was telling me something.

The next morning I was woke up with sausage, eggs, and biscuits with a glass of orange juice. This tray was good and hot too. By this time I knew how to move and eat with one hand cuff to the bed. "Are you feeling better Mr. Buckner?" "Yeah I could be feeling much better without this handcuff on me." "Well you will be leaving shortly." That was good news because by this time I was now worried about the stuff in my locker.

The transportation officers walked into the door I knew they was transportation officer because. They had chains and locks in there hand. "Buckner have you calm down?" "Are you feeling much better?"

"Yeah I am feeling much better now." I played it off like I had been giving medicine that made me feel much better. Truth be told I want feel better until I get home.

The one guard with the key to the handcuff that I had around my wrist unlocked me. He had my belongings in a bag. He handed them to me I grab my bag and walked to the restroom to get dress. After getting dress the transportation officer put the locks back on me. Now I was walking out of the hospital headed back to Terre Haute prison.

On the van I did the same thing going riding back as I did leaving. I wanted to see every object out both windows. Looking at people thinking they do not know how bless they are to be free. Wish it was me driving, wish it was me walking down the street, and I wish it was me eating in that fancy restaurant you people are in. Freedom what a wonderful thing.

It was over I could see the Terre Haute prison sign in the distance. Damn it was ugly! Pulling up at the old 75 year old prison made me sick to my stomach. All I was thinking was back to the dungeon. Now that I was here in front of the entrance door. My thought process was I am on my way to the SHU, but that was not the case.

My unit team just placed me in M-unit I did not get a write up/ shot for my misbehavior either. Being placed in M-unit was a punishment within it self I was already missing K- unit. It was all dark in the television room. The unit was all dim because some of the ceiling lights were broken out.

M-unit was an environment I did not want to stay live in. Just the few seconds of looking around I had already made my mind up to put in a cell change to get move back to K-unit.

When I walked in my new cell 006 lower I could tell that the prisoners that was living here was a nasty man. It was cloths, papers all on the floor. His bed was not made up, and it was laundry bags lying on the floor.

Look at it this way. It looked like a tornado came in and rip the whole damn cell apart.

I took action and started cleaning up the area where my stuff was gone go. First I cleaned off my sleeping area. All the items I thought were trash I through in the trash. All the items I thought the man forgot that was just living in the cell I put on the locker. It was stuff like old books, pencils, and pictures ripped out of old magazines. Stuff he really should have put in the trash with.

After a few minutes of cleaning up my area of living a big fat bold headed dude walked in the cell. "What's up big homey," he said. "My name is Oso" I put my hand in a fist then gave him a pound. Another prisoner with some glasses on walk in the cell too. He started picking up stuff that I had put on the locker I walked out because the cell is too small for three prisoners to be in.

Plus I wanted him to get all his stuff out my way. It was strange to me that both of them walked in the cell a few seconds apart. Stuff like that is a sign to me.

While waiting on him to get all his stuff I walked to the unit office to get me a cell change form. It was also strange to me that the man was moving out the cell that I was now in. He had move two doors down I seen. That was a sign to me too. What problem was the two having with each other? What did these people get me into by moving me to M-unit in this cell?

Man when I tell you cell 006 was disturbing. It was DISTURBING! The first thing I found disturbing about living with Oso. He likes to stay up all night watching television yelling out the door to other prisoners about what they were watching. Then on top of that he farts out loud. His bed was broke when he got in his bed it mad a loud sound. Every time he moved around the bad made the loud sound.

How long am I gone have to stay in this cell before I get move? I was asking myself. It was too much already I could see. The problems could be seen a mile awhile living in this cell and I have not been in here a whole day.

The next morning I woke up ready to eat breakfast. Then get back to the cell so I could get some more sleep. While waiting for the unit officer to call mainline I waited in the Television room. It was a totally different unit then K-unit. The computers were on the opposite side of the wall then K-unit. The Televisions had a lot of static in the picture, and it was no light in the room. The room was a cave compare to K-unit Television room.

"Mainline" the unit officer called out. Everyone started getting up walking to the Mp3 player charger to place their device on it I was one of them prisoners. M-unit was last to be call for mainline. The Down South table was full this day. The reason being biscuit gravy was on the line this morning. This was that breakfast on the compound. When I tell you the cafeteria is overcrowded it is a fact. It is a dangers time too. It is more prisoners standing around, and walking around in the cafeteria on the days Country breakfast is on the line.

In the line I was watching prisoners from the Down south table leave. I was hoping a seat would be open for me once I got there, but it was not. It was only one Down South table in the whole cafeteria with about seventy or eighty Down South prisoners. So I had to take a seat at the Kansas City & Missouri table. My plan was to move to my original table fast once a man got up. I did not want a prisoner to walk up saying I am in his seat I was not gone move until I got finish eating my meal. Luckily that did not happen and I got finish eating before a man from Kansas City or Missouri needed a seat.

Still sleeping I walked back to the cell. Then jump in bed. Not a good fifteen minutes into my sleep. "Bruce I forgot to tell you every morning I always use the toilet." Even though I did not want to get up out of bed. It was a rule unspoken if a man got to use the toilet. Or need some alone time in the cell. Give him the time he need/want.

I grabbed my headphones jumped off my bunk. Went and got a seat in the television room. On one television the news was on. The other television ESPN was on. My mind was not on watching television I was thinking what kind of time was this guy I was living with on. It was a whole hour before he walked up on me to let me know he was finished.

He said it again "I use the toilet every morning after breakfast." On the weekends I cook and sale fried burritos too. The room is jumping with guys coming in and out placing orders."

Really I was too tired. My mind was clouded I did not get enough sleep last night. What he was telling me went in one ear right out the other. Basically I ran back to the room to get back in bed.

It was around 9:00 A.M when I woke back up I did my usual routine. As if I was still in K-unit brush my teeth then wash my face. After getting myself together for the morning I decided I wanted to buy some new songs for my Mp3 player. When I walked in the room the computers was full. The computers could be used for a few different things. It is a form of communication to the outside World with emails. It is use to work on criminal cases. Prisoners look up different laws that have changed or either pass. That will help their case out. Personally I did not know laws change constantly as they did. Plus I was not all into the law like some prisoners are.

"Who next on the computer," I ask? No one said anything. The guy on the first computer got up. This was my first time getting on a computer in M- unit I found out I was not able to connect my Mp3 player up to the computer I chose. The reasoning being I had the new Mp3 player. The computer did not have the plug I could use. So I got up to get on another computer. Before I took a seat I looked at the connection. The last computer had the connection I needed.

The first thing I looked at after putting my pin number in was my account balance. A few hundred is what I so. That made me feel good right there I had to load up on songs after seeing my account. This morning I bought 600 links which is 30 dollars. With 300 links I could buy 15 songs.

Just to name a few rappers I supported Boosie Badazz Set It Off, Rick Ross Port Of Miami, 50 cents remix I Get Money, Gucci Mane Ridiculous , C-Murder Ghetto Ties, and Trey songs ft. T.I. 2 Reason. The last song I supported was to remind me how I felt in the club.

The unit counselor was not in the office at the time I wanted to talk to her. It was no way I was gone stay in this unit a long time if it was up to me. All I cared about at the time was putting in the effort into moving back to K-Unit. When she finally walked into the unit I was at her door. We had a talk. Into the conversion she told me I will have to find a cell open in K-unit before she would process my cell exchange form.

The weekend was in two days I really wanted to be gone by then. All that traffic coming to the cell I was not with that. Too many prisoners coming to the room was not good I had a lot of stuff that they could possibly steal. It was over 50 dollars' worth of soap, lotion, grease, and toothpaste sitting on my shelve. I did not want other prisoners to know what I got, and counting my pockets. Everybody be so damn shiesty. A customer might want to steal something to see how I will react.

That is how prisoners do. Let me still something to see how he will react. Even the man you doing time with in the cell will set stuff up. Just to see how you will react when something comes up missing.

Saturday morning at breakfast I had seen my new cell partner walk out with a bag of hamburger meat. He had a plug in the kitchen. It was a good hustle selling burritos. A new taste will sale. Fried burritos were something new to me. Think, Think, and Think of something you can come up with. Back in the unit it was a crowd of prisoners at the cell. When I walked up one prisoner said, "Make sure you have three for me."

Oso told him that he will start cooking at 3:30P.M, but I got you.

It was no use for me going back to sleep this morning I stayed out the cell. Until the guard said it was count time. Being in the cell with Oso was messing up how I do my time but I know how to adjust myself. It was no going home I got to buckle down and deal with how life in Terre Haute is being dealt to me.

In the cell I and he talk. The conversion was all about lifting weights. He said that he was the strongest man in Terre Haute with a bench press of 495 pounds. That is a lot of weight compared to my 295 pounds on the bench I told him I want to get up to 315 pounds on the bench.

"This is what I will do for you Bruce." "Start coming out on the yard with me and my boys." Monday-Friday after the 4:30 P.M. Count." "One thing my boys do not like is a lazy man, so you gone have to put some work in Big Homie." "If you work we will get you pushing 315 pounds on the bench press. In a little bit of time." That was the beginning of our cell friendship.

Doing count time I went to sleep. When I woke up it was around 10; 00 A.M it was nothing to do but watch some television, but everything that was on was boring. So I walked out the television room to go sit in front of the Caucasian television. Mountain Man was on. That was more of my style. I could learn something at the same time. It was not like I was just wasting my time. Getting some type of message out what I do day after day keep me motivate to make it to the next day.

Time came around for Oso my celly to cook his burritos. All the ingredients he use was on top of the locker hamburger meat, rice, green peppers, onions, and cheese. From the look of the ingredients the burritos will taste good. "How much do you sale the burritos for?" "One dollar twenty five cents." "I want three of them." No Bruce we cell partners. What I look like charging you."

At this time of conversion I was on my bed reading the new Hip Hop weekly. Oso was at his locker chopping the onions, peppers up. He also had his fryer heating up. The fryer was a small trash can with a stinger sitting at the bottom of the trash can. Note: A stinger is a heating tool that is made to boil water or in Oso case grease.

He pulled out a bust tub that was under his bed. The tube was full of ice, eggs, and cold drinks. "Bruce I use the top bunk to lay my burritos on" "It will not be a mess or nothing like that when I am finish" The doors were popping open at this time. So I jumped off my bed to find someone to play some chest with. It was a few guys sitting at the tables playing. I took a seat at one, and said "If it is aright with you two I would like to get next."

"Yeah you can get next." one of the guys said. "Do you know how to play?" "Yeah I can play, might be one of the best in the unit." I lied about being one of the best. It was just to get him hype about playing me.

How the chess table is ran in M-unit the players play the best out of five. The first person to three wins I just watch the two play until one wins. It was no talking. The two just played in silence. It looked boring to me. Me personally I like a little aggression on the board.

The game was over. The man with a wild Mohawk on top of his head won. When I got in front of the board he looked around. Then said "I got to be careful I got beef with a lot of prisoners in the BOP." When he said that I knew he was from Jamaica. While we were playing I was observing the prisoners walking in and out of my cell.

It was a whole lot of costumers that my celly was cooking for. Not really paying close attention to the moves being made on the board, I did not win a game playing the Jamaican. "You got a serious game Jamaica," I said after the five games.

He ask me what was my name. Bruce I said after telling him my name. He said he go by Bogus. It was a weird name to say so I told him I will call him Jamaica.

It was too much traffic at my cell so I got up from the chess table and walked to my room. When I walked into the cell it was a lot of smoke from the fryer. My bed was flipped with a trash bag laid flat on the bunk, with 60 burritos ready to fry. Another prisoner walked in and said he wants five of the sixty burritos that were lying on top of my bunk. He looked at me and did not say anything. It almost made me check the man.

That looking me up and down gets my blood to boiling. Too much smoke started to fill the room so I left back out. The unit was so boring I wanted to walk over to my old unit to chill. But I decided not to I did not want to mess up my chances of getting move back over there. It would be a headache if that was to happen. Having a headache in prison is not good. It will cause your behavior to change in a bad way. Later in the book you will read

After the 3:30 count I went to get my Mp3 player off the charger. It was not there I got upset about that. The first thing I did was go back to my cell. To look around and make sure my eyes are not playing tricks on me. Nope it was not in the area where I know I would have place it. So a prisoner got my Mp3 player.

My thought process was damn now I am on my way to the SHU for fighting the man that got my MP3 player. That was my only thought that came to mind. What made me feel better? It was this action that I took I grab somebody else Mp3 player off the charger.

The reason being I did not want to crash out. Plus I wanted to see how another man was gone react about his Mp3 player missing. Reader: See how prison got a good man thinking?

Back to my story: After about an hour had past my Mp3 player still did not come up. So I yelled out in the unit. "Do anybody have the wrong Mp3 player!" No one spoke up. My blood was really boiling now I paid 90 dollars for my Mp3 player I was thinking someone stole it to use for extra parts. That is what happens when an Mp3 has been taking. If mine did not come up I was gone start a chain of reaction.

A whole 3 hours had pass before this white boy came to my cell with my Mp3 player. When he gave me mine I gave him his. He went to tell some prisoner in the Indian car. The man came to my cell talking.

"M-unit does not tolerate stealing." Then I was like "if my Mp3 player comes up missing I will take someone else Mp3 player every time." "He did not know that he had your Mp3 player until 5 minutes ago." "You took his on purpose." "Check this out!" "Every time I than mistakenly took someone else Mp3 player." "It was back on the charger in no time." "By him having my Mp3 player for all those hours made me mad." "You need to tell him to be more careful." The conversation ended on that note.

The past few weeks been kind of good I sold my old Adidas. To one of the new prisoners that came in last week. I gave the Mexican a deal .Which was 18 dollars for the shoes. Commissary had 4 new pair of shoes that was in stock this week.

This quarter I was gone ball I walked up to commissary and bought two pair of shoes at the price of 80 dollars apiece. While walking down the hallway all eyes was on me. It was two pair of Nikes in my laundry bag. This prisoner in K-unit seen me and said. "Bruce I see you spending your limit up this month." Just so you can have an idea where the man was coming from. Terre Haute has a spending limit of 360 dollars a month. And I sometimes am at commissary every week in some months.

It was nothing for me to say I was already feeling myself. Back in my cell I put my new shoes in my locker. With my shoes in mind I made plans to take some picture this weekend.

With some old picture tickets I bought a couple weeks back. By me making plans this weekend I knew I had to go to the barber shop. For a fresh cut. And I had to get my prison fit iron for the weekend.

The frame of mind I had. Was like that thought when a boss got them fresh cloths just to party at the club.

Today is Friday I went up to the barber shop for a cut. My barber already had a person in the chair. That made me mad because I had already paid him 2 dollars for this time slot. When I got in the chair I had to get what I had on my chest on life, and told him. "My man I will never pay you first for a haircut again!" "My man you knew I was coming to get my haircut, I do not want to be waiting after I have already paid you my money!"

"City Boy I got a schedule I am on." "You have been doing time longer than me." "You should know better city boy"

Early I exercise my chest super hard. The reason being today this is Saturday. Is the day I will be stepping on the prison yard in my new shoes I bought last Tuesday.

After the 3:30 count I took me a long hot shower. I always want to be fresh in my pictures. Taken pictures are like getting a visit to me. In the visit room it always is a few pretty women. I want to look my best and look unstressed for my people. And you know it want be a good look for me if a woman I know from the streets. Seen me looking dirty the first time she seen me in years. The first impressions mean a lot.

Plus I knew once I sent the pictures out a lot of people will see me. That first impression I want the women my mother might show to have of me. Is this man on this picture is handsome. So being well groom is a must.

Walking out to the rack yard it is always a crowd heading in the same direction I made sure not to walk close to anybody I did not want to put my hands on no body. If my shoes were stepped on because it was gone be a problem if it happens. If it was an accident or not I was going to the SHU about these Nikes for real. So I kept a distance between me and other prisoners.

When I finally got on the yard where the picture man was it were other prisoners taking pictures at the time. It was a group of Caucasian guys taking a lot of pictures I could tell I think they was the Dirty White Boys. Not for sure, but they showed out with the pictures. They took the picture man to the grass to the wall. When all was said and done the Caucasian took 30 pictures.

After the Caucasian prisoners walked off satisfied at all of their pictures I walk up on the picture man because it was my turn. He had an attitude because the Caucasian had worn him out with all the walking. All I wanted was 10 pictures taking. First I wanted to take a picture playing chess.

Giving off the expression of deep thought, but I did not see any person I knew.

"Take one of me exercising on the bench press machine." "Terre Haute rule was prisoners cannot take pictures by or around the weight pile." He said back I did not believe him when he told me that because prisoners are lazy. My thought was he did not want to do anymore walking, but I took his word for it.

"Where can I take pictures at then?" "Places where the fence cannot be seen." "Okay take one picture of me kneeling on the grass." "Alright take another one of me posting over here on the bleachers" I pulled out my Mp3 player so I could listen to some music while looking at my surroundings while the picture is snapped, but the picture man said "Terre Haute want allow that either. "Pictures cannot be taken with any devices showing." He said to me.

At this point I really wanted to get smart with him because I was starting to think. He might have been fucking with me. He might was not though so I just let it go.

I started to feel bad blood boiling in me the picture taken needed to be over with before I started thinking in a real real negatively way. So I just started taking pictures anywhere. Such as

posting on the wall, sitting on the bench in front of the outside rec office. With my gray sweat shirt tied around my neck feeling like I had to think like a college student to get pass the bad thoughts. Jewel: Turn negative thoughts into positive ones

After I was done he ask me did I like all the pictures I had taken. "No" I said pointing out the ones I did not like. So yeah I took the couple pictures over.

When all was done with the pictures such as paying my ten tickets I went back to my cell to take my shoe off.

Something I learn to do in prison was budgeting the belongings I owned. So I made sure to make the money on my account, commissary, and shoes last as long as possible. One never knows when the storm will come. Living on a budget one will always have something and want have to ask any person for nothing besides supporting a thought or a product.

Today which is Monday I am not sure what the date is because I stop looking at the calendar, but on this Monday I went out for the first time to exercise with the Chicago car. The move was over and all the guys were standing around the bench press machine. One thing I took notice of. All of them were built. It was motivation to me. They had the size I want to reach do not get me wrong I am built too.

Before we started exercising I told them my name was Bruce. For the record the word on the compound was a man cannot be in the Chicago car without showing paper work, but it did not go that way with me. No one ask where my paper work was at. One man did ask me what kind of case I had.

"A pistol case" I said. All of the guys in the Chicago car introduce there self to me, After knowing what kind of charge I was lock away for. The old Muslim guy that I was in the cell with when I first arrive at Terre Haute. Was a top dog on the compound plus in the Chicago car. We were not in the cell that long to talk about were each other was from, but I found out this day that he was from Chicago. Plus a big dog. He said was up to me. Of course Oso spoke up "I told Bruce he could exercise with us. He said he want to reach 315 on the bench press I told him we can get him there."

The way the Chicago car had their routine going the weakest man go first ending with the strongest man. Since I was new the guys in the car wanted to know where I max out at on the bench." The most I had lifted was 255" I said to the man watching the weight behind me. Two other man put two 45 plates on the bar which was just my warm up weight. Before I showed were I max out at.

After that I was ready for the 255 pounds I lift the weight 5 times. All that exercising paid off I had got stronger. The first time I tried 255 pounds one lift was almost too much. That five I lifted had me ready to max out on some man.

After the Chicago guys figure out how strong I was. To my surprise I was stronger than two men in the Chicago car. That made me third in line to get under the weight. For the record third in line will be my spot until I get stronger. My spot can change if another man weight goes up or down.

Man when I tell you these guys were strong it is the truth. Some of the guys were in the low four hundred clubs. My cellmate Oso was in the high four hundred club I found out he was the strongest man on the compound.

By me finding that out I just knew I would reach the three hundred clubs. Oso had me cooking up boils with 70g of protein I was eating the bowls faithfully too. Sometimes we were in the cell drinking raw eggs together working I just drunk five eggs which I have never done in my life. The five eggs took me ten minutes to get down. Oso was drinking twenty eggs I tell you he would sit in his chair watching television. Cracking one egg at a time in a cup, and drink the twenty eggs in about 2 minutes.

It was not long before I was lifting more weight. It was a different exercising system then the Down South car system which got me bigger. Arm down which is Tuesday was when I really got it in with my city boys. First we warm up our arms on the pull up bar. Each one of us do 10 pull ups. Then 50 back arms. In all we do 10 sets. Add it up.

After the warm up we do skull crushes. Which I really like, this particular exercise we placed thirty five pounds on the small bar to start off. Each individual do two sets with the thirty five pounds weight. Then it really got serious the

Chicago men put two more thirty five pound weights on. One hundred seventy five pounds skull crushes. With that amount of weight I got big.

In time I got stronger than three men in the Chicago car. This was and felt like an accomplishment. My bench went up to 295 pounds when the three of them fell down to 255. The reason I past them every day I was on the wreck yard. Rain, sleet hail, and snow. Missing a day was a no, no in my prison sentence I was determine to stay fit with strength and have the same drive toward my body for the rest of my life.

Being the only man from Down South I was showing out my strength at times because they skip days, and I did not. I would tell them there body was not built for this type of punishment. My body was.

It was all motivation to them from me. It was to motive them to be at wreck no matter what. Lifting weights was like getting money. They were saying they were getting money, but they were falling off the weights. One has to work hard at it. Put in the proper work for the money one want to earn. Same goes for lifting weights. The work one put in the bigger one muscles will grow. It was also motivation for living back in the free world too.

This was a day the new Hip Hop Weekly hit the unit. Not for sure who was on the cover, but every time a new Hip Hop Weekly comes in the unit. Every prisoner that likes to read it want to see what is going down in the new magazine I know I do.

My cell buddy Oso got the magazine from one of his partners. I being in the cell I got to read it before a lot of guys. Oso read the magazine too, but did not give it back to his partner. It was sitting on the locker for a few days. Remind you Oso got a lot of his partners and friends that come in and out the cell all the time. Even when he is not in the cell some of them come and get stuff out not telling him.

One night I was on my bunk before the final lock down reading the second part of the Coldest Winter Everything by Sister Souljah. One of his partners came in and put the Hip Hop Weekly in his pants. He said "Bruce do not tell him I got the magazine I will place it back in the cell tomorrow." "Man I do not have anything to do with what you doing."

"Do not put me in it!" "That is your home boy." With that said I got back into the book I was reading when the unit officer calls lock down. Oso was one of the last prisoners to enter the cell.

Was not long before he seen that the Hip Hop Weekly was missing from on top of his locker. "Where is my magazine Bruce?" "Way you asking me last time I touched that magazine was when you let me read it." "That was a few days ago."

"It was right here on my locker when I left the cell." "All your partners are running in and out the cell." "One of them probably walks in the cell sometime today." "Me I have no idea where the magazine is Oso" "Do not ask me no more because I might start feeling some type of way."

Two of our cell door windows were broken out. Oso holler out the door for the rock man to come to the cell. Which is his Vice lord homeboy from Chicago. He walks up to the door and I could hear Oso ask him did he have the Hip Hop Weekly.

69

The answer was no. Oso then ask him to walk to all of the homeboys that he know that's always coming into the cell.

The prisoner that got the magazine was just in the left cell next door.

The rock man did not walk to that cell to see if that man had the magazine I was thinking he probably right on his bunk reading the magazine. Oso yelled out in the unit mad "who got my mother fucking Hip Hop Weekly!" I was thinking the city boy was gone stand up to say he got the magazine because he could hear Oso was mad.

He never spoke up on my behalf. Now at this time in the cell it is tension between me and Oso. Now can you see the picture I am painting for you? The prisoner that got the Hip Hop Weekly knows and hears what is going on in the cell. I see where his anger was going. It was pointing at me. I spoke up "do not think at all that I gave the magazine away I have nothing to do with your Hip Hop Weekly missing. " It was not my Hip Hop Weekly." "My homeboy let me keep that magazine." Oso said.

The next morning the prisoner that came and got the magazine out the cell was worry about putting the magazine back unnoticed. While Oso was in the room doing his morning routine I was watching television the guy that was responsible for the magazine confusion. Ask me to give the magazine back to Oso. "No I have nothing to do with what you did. " You should have spoken up last night." "By you not speaking up you put my time on the line." "I and Oso almost got into a fight over you playing." "You must have been scared to speak up" I said. Nothing was said from him.

Oso walked out of the room then went over by the exit door where all his homeboys were sitting. It looks to be a gang meeting. Yeah they were having conversation about what is gone happen to the thief. When he and other prisoners in the unit find out who got the Hip Hop Weekly. It was a zero tolerance for stealing.

From the corner of my eye I saw the guy throw the magazine in the cell. I got up from watching television to see where the magazine landed at in the cell I pick the magazine up. Which I shouldn't have and place it on Oso bed. When it was time for lock down I made sure I was second to walk in the cell.

When I walk in Oso had the Hip Hop Weekly in his hand. "Did you put the magazine on my locker?" "No" I lied. It was still tension between us because he knew I knew who had the Hip Hop Weekly the whole time. It did not matter how he felt about me I am not a rat I was not gone never say I knew the prisoner who took it. I did feel some type of way because I do not lie

Before the doors pop open the rock man walked up on the cell door. He asks Oso to come to the window. Something was whisper to him I could see whatever was spoken to Oso made him mad. He started putting on his back brace his work boots, and his weight lifting gloves.

When the doors pops open he walks to the cell next door I was fast on my feet. Being in prison as long as I have I knew something was about to happen. I was right too. When I walked out the cell I heard Oso arguing with the prisoner next door.

It was about walking in the cell and taking the Hip Hop Weekly without his permission. The guy that stole the Hip Hop Weekly was sitting on the bad saying we do not have to do this. You would not believe what came out of his mouth. He said "Bruce knew I got the Hip Hop Weekly. " Way you tell him I knew you took it. "He scared you into telling him that? I and Oso look at each other. I was not scared to fight in my sentence.

All I was thinking I am not a rat. Oso put his attention back on him. He was saying "we do not have to do this." His hands were in the air like he was gone block Oso punches. A fight did not break out between the two.

Since it was no fight I walked off to get me a seat in the television room. To think about what just happen. He told Oso I knew he had walked in the cell and walked off with the Hip Hop Weekly.

"Rat!"

I said to myself. Now I know me and Oso got a problem. It was not that serious to me. So I did not worry about how I was gone handle the problem.

When I was in thought this prisoner I never talk to walk up and took a seat beside me, and ask "What went on in that cell about that magazine?" "Word around the unit is Oso had him scared." He was surprise a fight did not break out between the two too. The one that had the Hip Hop Weekly always walks around like a tough guy with his white beater on showing his muscle. "Whatever you heard take it how you want to," but I am not about to put my word on it.

The guard calls out "chow time" I did not feel like walking down to the cafeteria to eat I was thinking how will I make a move.

Some way I need to get out of cell 006. The way I am and how I do my time a fight will break out. It was already tension between the two of us. By scary dude telling him I knew he took the magazine. He got something to fight with me about. It was a lie

It all worked out in my favor since Oso being in the unit for four years. He had a lot more pull then I did. He had been working on a move the whole time since the magazine was stolen. While I was watching television he was in the office talking to the counseling about moving me to another cell which was his homeboy cell, the rock man. She put the paperwork in right then and there. Right before the final lock down my name was on the list for cell exchange.

Like I said before it worked out in my favor when I move to my new cell which was upstairs cell 277. The man was cleaner and neater than Oso was.

The first night in 277 upper I just lay in my bed reading my book. He was my fifth cellmate in Terre Haute. He was a laid back quite type I looked down from reading my book. He had his paperwork out reading and going over his case I could see "If you mind telling me how long you been locked up?" "Ten years on a life sentence." "Damn" I said, I thought about asking him what kind of case did he have, but didn't.

The following morning I woke up to my regular routine. Use the toilet as always, brush my teeth, and wash my face. Walk down to the television room set down in a chair in the back ready and waiting for chow to be call. It was not long after I took a set for the guard to yelled chow time.

When I walk out the unit I bump into my partner from the Therapeutic Community program. "What is up Bruce?" "How is it living in M-unit?" "I am going through it homeboy!" he said. "That program tough I was in one 2007- 2009 a place called Corrections Corporation of America back home in Nashville, Tennessee I said back. "The way it is set up a man got to tell on another man." "Then that start a problem with in the program." "Yeah that is how it works." "But I got to do what I got to do for me." "In nine months I will be home with my three daughters."

Inside the cafeteria at the table the homeboy from Louisville, Kentucky was sitting at the end seat.

When I caught his eye I mugged him. The reason being him and another homeboy from New Orleans, Louisiana got into a fight the other day; I do not think it is right to fight the homeboys. If something pop off on the compound between the Down South car and another car. We need to link up and run the other car off the compound.

Then on top of that word was told to me that the Kentucky boys gang homeboy from Louisiana. When I got to the table I spoke up. "What is up with you ganging or fighting the homeboy? " No it was not like that." "Then break it down to me then!" I said." He stated a watch came up missing in the unit." "Homeboy from Louisiana had found the watch, but did not return the watch to the rightful owner. The man that lost the watch had signs staple to the wall stating that MY WATCH MISSING PLEASE RETURN TO CELL 255. Homeboy had the watch. He comes to me asking if I knew any one that will buy the watch. Hell no I said."

Men that steal I do not like. By me not liking what he did I told the guy in the other car he had the watch." "When it got back to homeboy he walked up to me and calls me a rat. Bruce I do not play that name calling." We had to fall in the room about that."

"The reason he said we gang him; while we was fighting he ran out the room. Lil homeboy pushes him back into the cell to me." It was no ganging involved."

Living in cell 277 doing time was not as bad as I thought. At first I thought It was gone be a problem with the move. He being from Chicago plus being Oso homeboy. All we did was eat, sleep, and shit in the cell. As for me and Oso having tension between the two about the Hip Hop Weekly being taken he never said anything about it. It was never too much talking to each other, and he never got in my space I never got in his space.

Plus for the first time in my bid locking down was not bad. By him being the rock man the cell door did not lock. It was always slightly open. By the door being like that I always felt a little free in the cell.

One day while I was taking a nap the counseling from K-unit knocked on my cell door. "Buckner come on pack your stuff you are moving back to K-unit." At first I did not know if I was seeing what, I really was seeing it was a woman I like at my cell. Was I dreaming?

By me not knowing I laid my head back down. For the record; I had always had dreams of women knocking on my cell door telling me to come on.

She said it again "Buckner come on pack your stuff you are moving back to K-unit." "If you want you can stay over in this unit." At first I was thinking about staying it was alright living in cell 277, but I thought about how much better it was living in K-unit. Now back in K-unit my location was cell 087 lower. Walking in the cell I had the top bunk again.

The man living in the cell was not present at the time of my arrival. When I start to place my stuff on my shelve. OG Rust walked in the cell. The first thing he say to me "I got a homeboy that already had a moving sheet in he at the other end of the hallway. So you need to find another cell that is open." I knew he was lying but I said" Okay." I knew he had seen me go crazy on the joint I had smoked a couple months back. Because of that situation he did not want to be in the cell with me. He will tell me that later on.

OG Rust one of them old timers. That has been to prison more than three times. These types of prisoners are call convicts. Everything is taking serious. Respect is the number one rule. Second rule straightening another man at the first misunderstanding between one another, and if another misunderstanding happens one of us got to go because the third time I am dangerous.

Any way I did not like the tension he was putting off. Once I put all my belongings up I went out to find an empty cell that I could possibly move in. I walked around and look inside every cell in the unit. Not one was empty I walk to the unit office to get me a cell exchange form. Because it was a few cells that had one man living in it.

Really I did not want to go through the problems of asking another man will you let me move in the cell with you. A man wants to have the cell to his self as long as possible. By asking another man that, I was just setting myself up to hear no. I decided against asking a man that question. If Og Rust wanted me to move he has to put the work in for the move.

After making my decision I went in the television room. The Down South chair was right in front of the TV, I did not sit there for some reason. It was a chair in the second row at the end. That I like to sit in too so that is where I took a seat.

A move was call all the cars was walking back in the unit from wreck. Some guys walked in the television room before taking a shower. Just to get on the computer to read new emails. See if there money hit the account.

"Bruce Bruce is you back over here?" "Yeah man I am back over here." "Bruce you are crazy what were you on that day?" "I had smoked some weed." "Who cell are you in?"

"OG Rust cell," "What did he do when he found out you was in his cell?" "He told me he had a partner that was supposed to get move in the cell before I came." "That it was a mistake that I was move in the cell." This prisoner from Chicago name Icky walk in. "Bruce you back?"

"Do you have some of that green you was smoking on that day?" In a matter of fact I do have a joint in my property I had bought three days ago for 2 chili packs which is $1.65 each. Plus 14 stamps which are .49 cents a stamp I did not want to get in any more trouble. So I afford the joint for sale.

"If you want it give me 10 dollars!" It is Kush! "Let me see how it looks?" We walked down to my cell. When I pull the joint out the smell of the Kush took over the room. "Yeah that is some Kush." "How much did you say again?" I said $15 dollars city boy!" I thought you said $10 dollars." "Give me $10 dollars City boy."

I did not make a profit I just needed to get it out of my possession.

"Wait a minute I am going to see if Sixty(a prisoner name) will go half on the joint with me." "When the two prisoners come back to my cell their money was short, but I decided to let the two run with the joint. The two said I will get paid on store day.

"Bruce you in the cell with OG Rust," Icky ask before walking out the cell. Everyone knows OG Rust as the man that set all the way in the back chair with his fan plug up beside him, and If you look at him to long. He will check you by asking. What is up with you?

It was not long before I learn how OG Rust does his time. In the mornings around 4.00A.M the guard on the clock always comes open up our cell. Reason being OG Rust was the rock man in the hallway. All day he walks up and down the hallway sweeping, mopping, and emptying out the trash cans.

He also had a side hustle going. His side hustle was selling tobacco the kind of tobacco that goes in a person mouth. Then make the person spit. Every guard in Terre Haute uses this tobacco.

What OG Rust do is once the guards spit it out on the ground or through it in the trash. He will get the tobacco dry it out, then sale the dried out tobacco for $6 dollars a cigarette. He had been doing that for eight years now. One night we stayed up a few extra hours over our usual sleep time.

On this night we pulled out our paper work to show one another what we were in prison for I found out he had a pistol case like I did.

He told me this was his last time coming two prison. He also says when he get out he will be straight because he got over $20,000 thousand on his account. From selling the cigarettes he

been selling and he will make more because 4 years is left on his sentence . The day I walk out the door I will have just about or over $40,000 thousand on my account.

"Bruce the reason I told you I had a partner that was moving in the cell when you first came." "I saw what you do once you smoke a joint. You become crazy I did not want you to wake up in the middle of the night and kill me. That day you got high man that was crazy I never seen nothing like that before in my life."

I and OG Rust keep the cell very clean. One day doing count time this woman guard. Spoke to us through the broken windows. "You two have the cleanest cell I have seen so far" she said.

Every other day one of us cleans the cell. We had spray bottles full of bleach old rags to wipe the cell down, and the brush for the toilet. We also had a small broom with a dust pan. All of our stuff was neatly place in the area they belong.

We both knew if anything of ours was out of place or something was touch.

One day I was cleaning out my bowl after eating. All of a sudden I got sleepy. So I decided to take me a nap. This was around 2:00 P.M I also calculated that I will wake up around count time. Note: See how prison got my brain working? I was doing time counting time.

Falling asleep took only 15 minutes I found myself having a dream about. My girl I had when I was on the street. She was a thick spicy red bone. The dream consists of me asking her to marry me. She said yes to my proposal.

After that we made sweet love with one another. We were kissing looking each other dead in the eye. We had a beautiful life together. The attraction we had with one another could not be broken. The love we had was pure. The dream did not last very long around 3:50P.M I was woken up by OG Rust walking in for count time.

A few minutes later the guards walk around looking into the cell counting prisoners yelling out "COUNT TIME STAND UP!" Writing down every prisoner was seen alive doing the time that they had walked past there cell. "COUNT TIME STAND UP!" The guards was yelling a few doors down I could hear

The doors were open up around 5:00P.M which is a little late. "CHOW TIME" the unit officer yelled I decided to walk down to the cafeteria just to see what was serve. Today was alright chicken subs with chips was on the line I smashed the whole tray got up than walk back to the unit. Walks inside the television room got in a chair to watch the weekend movie.

Every weekend the institution play a new movie if I did not like the movie that was about to play on these days. All I had to do was go to the gym when the move was call, and pay the gym worker $2 dollars to put in a movie of my choice.

On the wall are over two hundred DVD movies. That Terre Haute has bought over the years like I said before it is a hassle getting to the television in the gym. Everybody is rushing to get to the best movie. This is how the television in the gym is set up.

Two televisions are playing the same movie another three television are playing the same movie. And another three are playing the same movie. After all them television sets are taken. It is three blank televisions that you could pay to sit at. The gym worker makes his money off these.

The movie that started playing I did not like. So when the move was call I rush to the gym even running a little bit. Still did not get a good television. So I decided to pay the gym worker. By giving him two dollars he walks in the back to grab the DVD of my choice, and turn on one of the blank television so I can watch. He a Caucasian man and the only man in Terre Haute with the key to the DVD movie locker he take pride in having the key. I looked at the list of DVD movies. Searching for a movie I have not seen found it.

"Gym worker go get Think Like A Man." He went in the back to get the movie. While he was searching for the movie I took a seat at the blank television. Real testimony I was feeling good. It felt like I just paid my way in a real movie theater. All I needed was a woman by my side, popcorn, and something to drink. While watching all the previews it was a great feeling flowing through my body. Knowing I am about to watch a movie that I been waiting to see for so long. At this moment I made my mind up to make coming to the gym on the weekend part of my schedule.

Sunday morning sun came up I gave my God praise. Letting him know I am thankful for him waking me up this morning and the past mornings. Yes I believe in God the

Father, the Son, and the Holy Ghost. After all the time I had did I stayed true to my God.

Even after reading about religion beliefs just for one kind of people. For instance one religion group that caught my eye was Islam. This religion is said to be for African American people. This guy name lil Mo introduce me to Islam.

One day he asks me if I wanted to learn something new. It was nothing else to do I agreed to learn what he wanted to show me. "What I got to show you is down in the chapel." That was a plus I will not turn down going to a chapel. Feeding my spiritual being is always good.

We walked down to the chapel. When we got through the doors he asks me to get two chairs while he walk to an office where stuff could be check out. I found a spot where we could sit. He walks up with a small DVD player with a small screen made with it. He said "this DVD will give you some history on African American roots. "Word" I said that got me excited learning some history. The DVD came on showing racism from back in the day.

That part of the African American history I did not want to learn about. But I kept watching to see was I gone learn something I did not know. A man came on the screen. He was in some city standing out. Asking different people a question. The question was. "What is your nationality?" Some people were saying Asian, American, and African American. When the person answer African American. He said "that is two continents.

You cannot be from two continents." Then he said "what I want you to know is that we are confused." "We the African

American people do not know what country we are original from.

It was some deep stuff he was saying. He also said "Christianity is not for African American people" "Caucasian people are using the religion to control us. " Caucasian people took our original names then gave us a new one. The way they did that was by whipping the African American with a whip if they every used there African name.

The Caucasian people wanted us to forget our original name. So we could not trace back to our real country. He said "If you want to break through the confusion do research to find out where you are original from.

Listening to that DVD was interesting, Lil Mo but I will never stop believing in the Father, Spirit, and the Holy Ghost. He said "how three gone make one?" Really I did not want to get into this conversation with him because I could go all day on this topic.

"Listen to this other DVD." "This is on how America was built." A whole hour had past and the DVD was not finish. All the prisoners in the back of the chapel were walking toward the door where I and Lil Mo were sitting. This was right in front of the exit door. That is how I knew an hour had gone past. We both started packing the stuff up at the same time. That was my first and last times every going to the chapel to watch a DVD.

In two weeks I had a meeting with unit team. The counseling sent me a remind you letter for my appointment. All I was thinking was it better be some good news. As far as I know I have not been in any trouble. The appointment had me a little nervous.

It was on a Thursday when I heard my name been call out by the counselor. She seen me walking to her office from a distance I walk in behind her. "Buckner your half way house papers are here for you to sign." "Thank you for working hard on my case." I said to the counselor.

After signing my papers my whole train of thought changes. My time was really almost over I been waiting so long to feel like this. The darkness was starting to lighting up a little. The pressure of waking up every morning did not seem as bad. Knowing I got my date. It been 4 ½ years I been away from home.

I walk to my room to let it sink in, but before I got comfortable. This prisoner knock on my door I am not good at remembering names. So I am gone call him Baltimore. "Bruce did you get a look at her fat pussy print." "Yeah I saw that fat pussy on her." "Did you get your half way house date?"

"That is my business. Yeah I just sign for my date!" Once I told him that. He started talking to me like a man. "Bruce do not get into a fight with any one." I have been in prison a long time over 15 years. In my 15 year prison bid I have seen different men lose their date."

" Do not lose focus on the big picture." "Some of these prisoners will never see the free world again." Believe me they do not want to see or hear about another man going home." "Get money when you get home!" Baltimore walks out my cell after telling me that.

The exact dumb stuff Baltimore spoke to me about minutes early to not to do I did the opposite. It happens in the gym. This is how it happens I jump off my bunk when the move was called. Walk to the gym to watch a movie I did not get the television I wanted as usually. One prisoner got up then left. It was the television I wanted so I got it.

This bank robber from Wisconsin walks in the room. He was a real lil man. Wisconsin was only 20 years old. Never been in trouble before being in Terre Haute was his first time being incarcerated in is life. We horse play together from time to time. He walks up to me and smacks me in the back of my neck. Sincerely I wanted to fight him just to school him how it is being incarcerated.

My blood pressure went from 0 to 100 in a second I got out of my chair and hit him in the eye. The fight lasted a few minutes after that the guard ran in to break us up. All I could think about was I then lost my half way house date. This fight happens December 6, 2015.

Terre Haute is a prison that automatic ship prisoners that have been in a fight. Me having last then 6 months go home. Terre Haute was not gone ship me. The bank robber from Wisconsin got ship within 65 days. He also left his radio to me. It was no bad blood between us.

It was March when I was let out the SHU. My unit team kicks me back out of K-unit and put me where I did not want to live M-unit cell 214 upper. This was an Ohio cell. A guy name Staff would now be my cell partner. We were on the wrong foot the first few days. The both of us had to feel each other out. Peep how one another do his time.

The reason Staff was on guard for the first few days. His man Reese which we both know said "if Bruce smoke some weed it will be an issue in that cell. He put him on edge by letting him know that.

Any way on my tenth day back in M-unit. This new cat from Tennessee came in. Me being me showed him some Southern hospitality I gave him a few items he needed. If he wear the same size shoe I wear I would have gave him a pair of shoes which he needed badly. Sometimes I regret being 100%.

On his third day in the unit I saw him at the chess table playing Jamaica drinking something in a bottle. "Bruce" he yelled out while I was walking down the unit to the phones. The phones were pack I saw from a distance so I took a seat at the chess table." "Do you want to sip on this white lighting with me?"

"Yeah" I grab the bottle out of his hand. Something inside of me was saying Bruce do not take a drink. Being hard headed I took 3 big sips.

Man when I tell you lighting struck me after about minute. It is the truth I was up on my feet wanting to fight every man that I had a misunderstanding with in the past. This pussy ass prisoner name Twan kept getting in between me and the opponent.

It was four prisoners talking to me saying "Bruce go to your cell to come down." "No I will fight all of you" I said to the four prisoners looking all of them in the eye. "Bruce chill out just go in your cell before the police come." "Fuck the police!" My partner Jamaica walks up to me with a root beer in his hand, and handed it to me, but I threw it to the floor.

"LOCK DOWN" the guard yelled out while walking to the middle of the unit. "LOCK DOWN" he said yelled.

Now I was in a cell turn all the way up on white lighting I could not stay in bed. The guard knew I had taken something.

"Buckner quiet down" the guard said. "Fuck what you are talking about I am not quieting down I am a got damn vampire. "Call a code Buckner is not gone calm down."

Five guards were at my cell door now. "Buckner have your hands to your side once this door is open. We are coming in to restrain you" the guard said. When the door was open I did what I was asked.

Back in handcuff again walking back to the SHU.

When we arrive in the SHU program area I was place in the holding cell with the bars. The guard asks me to give him all my clothing; I did what I was asked. Now I was in the cell ass naked for a few minutes. He finally came back with my clothing after searching them.

The second guard came up to the holding cell with a breathalyzer test for me to blow in. When I blew in the tester for some reason I thought I pass with flying color. That was not the case. Just from taken three big sips of prison made white lighting. The test stated I was intoxicated.

This was another stressful time in my life. My unit team was prolonging my shot for being intoxicated. The reason being I still had to have a team meeting about my half way house date. But nothing could be done with my shot not being handle. My team had to wait to see what the DHO team members was gone do with my case.

It was a whole three months before the situation was handle. On top of that I still was not told everything I needed to know.

But one morning the counselor knocks on my cell door with some papers in her hand. She opens the flap on my cell and sled the papers to me. "What are these papers I am about to sign?" "Those are your half way house papers." "Really I still got my date after all those shots I got?"

"Yeah Buckner you got the date. "We also need your fingerprint" People I was so excited I almost let her leave without telling me the exact day. "Ms. Taylor" I yelled out my cell door for her to come back. "What day do I leave for the half way house?" "July 16 Buckner" she said. That was just a few weeks away I thought.

But the day I was getting out the SHU to be put back on the compound. My date was taking. At the time I did not know what for. The guards that was working the range could not tell me way. It was strange that I was not getting release back to the compound. It had been three months. Me not knowing the whole time my points were going up. Now I was USP status.

The next morning is when I found this out. The guard working the range came to my door. "Pack your stuff Buckner you are getting ship." It totally caught me off guard. Now I was confused. The reasoning being I did not know was I still able to go to the half-way house July 16.

Now back to the shipping process. I with a few other guys was place in holding cells. "Bruce" this guy yelled out. "What is up?" "Who are you?" "Clay I was in the SHU with you the first time you came back here." "You have been back here the whole time I ask?" "Yeah I been back here six whole months Bruce." We had to wait until the guard got our property from out the back. The guards then placed our green army bags on the wall. That had our name tag hanging out of them. We were then ask to pick up our property and walk to the van.

We had no idea where we were going. It was me, Clay, and two Caucasian prisoners. It did not matter where I was going I was gone hold my own. Clay on the other hand was a little shaking up. He kept asking the guards where was we designate too. It was not long before he got his answer.

We were designate to the prison right across the street Federal USP Terre Haute. When we first walked in I notice how cold it was. This prison had an air & heating system. It was very new looking.

While we was getting book into the system I wanted to know if my date was in the Computer. In front of the desk I ask "Do you see a half-way house date for me?" The guard did not give me an answer. So I ask another question "Will my date be taken since I got ship over here?" Still no answer now I was anxious because the system is unpredictable on these kinds of situations.

As soon as I seen a different guard walk in the area where I could ask my questions I popped off, and ask the same question I was asking the first guards. Will my date be taken from me for getting ship over here?" The answer I wanted to know was not giving to me.

The only answer I was getting. You will have to get that information from your unit team.

Still in the booking process the guards place me plus the others in F1. While in F1 Gucci Mane name was ringing all over the compound. Guys were telling me Gucci Mane over on the other side in C building. Gucci Mane this, Gucci Mane a weirdo I laugh at the weirdo statement because he had a song that be banging (I'm A weirdo I'm weirdo).

When the booking process was over I was placed in unit A-2 when I first walked in cell 15 lower. The first thing I notice was that it was bigger than most cells. It smells like a hospital, and a man in a wheel chair was living in it. Please God I thought:

If my halfway house date was still in the computer I will be gone in a few weeks. So I really did not care who I would be in the cell with. All I had to do was stay to myself do my own thing, and go home. That will not be the case.

The man I will be in the cell with rolled into the cell. The first thing he ask me where was I from. "The medium from across the street" I said. He also asks me what car I was in. "The Down South car" I stated. "You in the car with Gucci Mane" he said "He down there in C-2." "Have you seen him I ask?" "Yeah Gucci Mane come to the cafeteria to eat every blue moon. The first few times I went to cafeteria Gucci Mane was not in there. The fourth day on the USP compound I walk pass a few guys that was like in the middle of the table. My seat that I chose to sit in was at the fare end. It was this prisoner sitting across from me. I ask him "Way Gucci Mane never comes to chow?" "There he go right there." He said. Gucci Mane was literally right beside me. I could not believe it was Gucci Mane the rapper. He had lost a lot of weight.

After being In USP Terre Haute for over a week I still have not spoken to unit team about my half way house date. One day while walking around the unit the counselor finally walks in. Her name was Mrs. Shoe I walks up to her. "Mrs. Shoe my name is Bruce Buckner I introduce myself to her first before speaking to her about my situation I did not want to come off as a trouble maker.

"It has been over a few weeks since I was shipped over here from right across the street. All I want to know is my half way house date in the computer?" "Yes Buckner your date is still in the computer she said back. That was a big relief for me.

Since I knew my date was in the computer I wanted to start some trouble.

Note: do not think like this when you are almost at your goal.

In my locker I only had a few commissary items plus on top of this I was on commissary restriction. It was this Asian store man that I met. My idea was to run my bill up until my half way house date. By getting all the items I will need to cook Fried rice. Just so you know fried rice is an $8 dollar bowl. Every day I was going to the Asian guy store.

The system hit me hard on July 16 the day I was to leave to the have way house. My name was not call for release. It was in the afternoon. Plus in the past I have seen other prisoners leave in the morning. Something was not right I walks to the unit office to ask the guard to look up my release date. It was a long wait at his desk, but only a few seconds. "January 26" he said I had lost my date again. It was not a good feeling after he told me this (Pause) I felt sick. That was 6 months away.

It was a call I had to make but did not want to, and the call was to my mother. I called to tell her my date was reset. This would not be the first time I told my mother bad news about me not coming home. On the phone she was like God then got you this fare. He will get you through 6 more months. After all it was a good call it felt a little better talking to my mother. So I man up took the set back like a man, and started Living Life in Terre Haute again.

Four months had pass since I found out my half way house date was reset I was on my way out the door again. So I thought. The day after my birthday November 12, 2015 I popped off again. I and this 43 year old man were having problems. We had got into a fight in the cell a few days ago.

The second situation started at the microwave. I was hungry with fried rice in my bowl when I walks to the microwave to cook my fried rice bowl. It was a three other men waiting to use the microwave like me. When I ask who was last the Caucasian man said he was.

The guy I got until the fight with walks up. Saying he was after the Caucasian. I not knowing his bowl was beside the microwave. Took it like he was trying to skip me. "Was his bowl really right there" I ask the Caucasian.

For some reason he did not say anything. It was not that serious at the moment. So I went to sit in my seat in front of the television, and wait for my turn on the microwave. Then dude that I got into a fight with walk close to where I was seated. He said something but I did not hear him clearly. "What the fuck did you say to me" I said. "If you got a problem me we can handle it when chow is call" That is what he said. Even though I was gone go to chow. He called me out. So I just stayed in the unit until it was clear. My ankle was sprung from the first fight. It was sprung so bad that I was walking on crutches.

My first thought was to crack his head so I went with that. When the rock man came down the stairs I ask him. "Where is the push broom?" "It is upstairs in the exercise room. "MAN I AM ABOUT TO CRACK HIS HEAD" the word flowed out my mouth. The rock man said "Bruce you not gone do nothing. He was wrong.

Now that I got the push broom I walks in my cell like I was about to clean up. What I was really doing was unscrewing the stick part off the dust catcher when I walks out of my cell. The old dude that said something I did not like. Was sitting by cell 028 eating his soup he had just cooked.

At this time I was walking toward him acting like I was sweeping trash up. When he looked at me it was too late I had swung the wooden stick at him. It made contact. He stood up trying to block the stick from hitting him. After the 7th swing the stick broke on him. He picks up pieces of the stick now trying to hit me with it. It was a chair close to me that I pick up to hit him with, but not before being surrounded by guards me not getting down on the ground when the guard told me to. He ends up pepper spraying me all in my face. The pepper spray did not affect me right off, but when I walked outside.

The air must have activated the pepper because I could not breathe. The guards walk me to a cell that had a shower in it.

The first thing I did was wash my face, but it got worse. The pepper spray was filling up my lungs I could not breathe! I thought I was gone die. It was that bad. After literally putting soap in my eyes to scrub the spray pepper out the burning stop.

Back in the SHU program I was moved in the cell with this gay dude from DC I did not know he was gay at first, I will get to that later, but any way the first few days went smooth. After my fifteen day it was time for cell exchange. This is when I found out he was gay. It was another gay prisoner from DC that moves in the cell right beside us.

The guy DC man in the cell with me knew him. One day while I was sleep he was on the door talking to the other DC dude. "Listen youngster I been a homosexual a long time. The best sex I have ever had was with a boy. When I was out I use to do my thing I had me a women with a punk on the side. When we would have fights I just went over my punk house for sex. See I been doing this a long time. One occasion I was with my puke we got freaky this night I was letting him stick his finger in my ass." I jumps up "Dude I do not want to hear that shit". It was no second guessing I put in a request form to be move to a different cell. He said "I want talk like that know more." The other gay dude next door always would start making connection with the DC punk in my cell. Then the gay talk would start all over again.

The only reason I did not hit him in the eye the first few times he was talking gay around me. My ankle was sprung real bad. On top of that I was planning on beating my shot by putting the fight on the other prisoner that came to the SHU with me.

My release from Terre Haute was on the line I needed to beat this Shot/write up. Plus not to get another shot/write up for fighting. The gay conversations the two was having was every other day. I wanted out of the cell. Every time guards walk down the range I would "say what is up with my cell exchange?" The guards never gave me an answer.

One morning I got up to sign up for wreck. The guards came to the cell at 6:00A.M to hand cuff me. Going outside in the SHU was something I did not like, but I had to get away from this gay prisoner. Since the unit manger did not move me out the cell. Taken matters in my own hands were my only choice.

When wreck was over I did not cuff up. The guards was being (pause how can I explain this) very talkative by saying "Buckner this is not the way." "Cuff up we gone put you in another cell." That was a lie. But I cuff up When I walking through the guards area. The lieutenant walks up on me with a problem, and said "put him back in the cell you got him from.

He know what he was doing was not right if a man refuses to go back in the cell with the other guy. As the lieutenant he supposed to find another cell to put the other man in. Just to keep the confusing down inside the cell.

As soon as they put me back in the cell I head butted him. The DC dude never saw the head butt coming the Lieutenant calls a code and I was taken out the cell.

Now I was placed down stairs in unit A. This unit right here was special. The doors had metal boxes on the slots.

Every prisoner in this unit had been doing something crazy.

I not knowing it was a set up from the guards let this Jamaican prisoner move in the cell with me. Before the craziness started he talks about how he was a Kingpin that have move tons of marijuana, all the money on his account. And that he have killed a lot of people in his life.

My conversation was on not having a woman to write while doing all this time. He then pulls out a pin pal brochure. Hands the brochure to me and say pick a plan. "For what" I said. "You want a woman to write. He then offers to buy me a pen pal for the year.

After all the talking what he did not tell me was that every year he goes through something where he stays up a whole week with no sleep, kicking on the door, breaking the sprinkles , and pissing on the floor I was trying to go home without any more setbacks. It took all I had not to do what I did to him, but to make a long testimony short he almost died in the cell with me. When he would not lie down and let me get some sleep from me telling I am sleepy. Again I took matters in my hands.

First I hit him with the tray I had. When he falls to the solid floor I kick his head all up against the wall. The last kicks were so hard his life stopped. He was laid out on the floor not moving. I thought he was dead I looked down to see if he was still breathing. He was so I jumps back on my bunk. And try to get some sleep.

Do not think I am pushing you to be like I was in prison because I am not. My goal is to stop you from experience a place like Terre Haute.

Diamond: Do something better with your life. Something positive that will help others that will come up behind you.

Christmas day was right around the corner. All we were waiting on was the special dinner Terre Haute would serve. Not so special when it came. The chicken was thick, tough and not cook to perfection in some places. The dressing was dry, and the eggnog was artificial. That was my Christmas in Terre Haute.

January came and I still had not been to DHO I still had two shot pending. Remind you that my release date for the half way house was January 26. By my shots still pending I will not be able to get release. Damn January 26 was right around the corner.

When January 26 did come it was one of the loneliest days of my life. The reason being I did not want to eat; I did not want to get out of bed. All I wanted was to get home. The world seems so quiet at the time. This was the day I should be walking out of Terre Haute to my freedom, but no I was lying on a bunk.

When the day was over I got back to feeling normal right back to doing time which was doing my bur-pees, push-ups, and back arms. That was my days in the SHU exercising my stress away.

BF-A0288
AUG 11

INCIDENT REPORT CDFRM

U.S. DEPARTMENT OF JUSTICE   FEDERAL BUREAU OF PRISONS

Part I - Incident Report

1. Institution	FCC TERRE HAUTE			
2. Inmate's Name BUCKNER, BRUCE	3. Register Number #20452-075	4. Date of Incident 11-12-2015		5. Time 5:45PM
6. Place of Incident A-2 DAYROOM	7. Assignment A2 ORD	8. Unit A2		
9. Incident: Assaulting any person, Possession of weapon, Fighting with another person, Refusing to obey orders of staff	10. Prohibited Act Code(s) 224,104,201,307			

11. Description Of Incident (Date; Time; Staff became aware of incident) 11-12-15 5:45PM

On above date and at approximately 5:45pm I S/O J. Kremitzki was returning to the unit from the crossover when I noticed I/m 24254-076 Mitchell, Darnell Fighting with I/m #20452-075 Buckner, Bruce in the unit dayroom. I/m Buckner was using a stick from a broom as a weapon and striking I/m Mitchell with it numerous times in the face and upper body. I/m Mitchell was using a chair and was striking I/m Buckner with it at his upper torso. I called for assistance as I ran over to the inmates and ordered them both to stop fighting and drop the weapon, both inmates refused. I turned to I/m Buckner an observed him reach down to pick up a broken piece of wood from the broom stick. I then gave him an order to drop the weapon as I presented my can of O.C and stated "Get down OC, OC. He then hit my right hand trying to knock my OC canister away from his direction. At this time I administered one (2) second burst of O.C. I then placed inmate Buckner on the floor with the least amount of force necessary and applied mechanical restraints. I/m Buckner was escorted by staff from the housing unit to be medically assessed as the rest of the unit was secured with no further incidents. This is a re-write from 11-12-2015.

12. Typed Name/Signature of Reporting Employee J.Kremitzki *[signature]*	13. Date And Time 12-15-15 7:00PM	
14. Incident Report Delivered to Above Inmate By (Type Name/Signature) J.Sherman *[signature]*	15. Date Incident Report Delivered 12-15-15	16. Time Incident Report Delivered 710 pm

Part II - Committee Action

17. Comments of Inmate to Committee Regarding Above Incident

[handwritten] 12-23-15   *[handwritten] 33 days*

[handwritten] 33 working days

18. A. It is the finding of the committee that you:
        _____ Committed the Prohibited Act as charged.
        _____ Did not Commit a Prohibited Act.
        _____ Committed Prohibited Act Code(s) _____

   B. _____ The Committee is referring the Charge(s) to the DHO for further Hearing.

   C. _____ The Committee advised the inmate of its finding and of the right to file an appeal within 20 calendar days.

19. Committee Decision is Based on Specific Evidence as Follows:

20. Committee action and/or recommendation if referred to DHO (Contingent upon DHO finding inmate committed prohibited act)

21. Date And Time Of Action _____ (The UDC Chairman's signature certifies who sat on the UDC and that the completed report accurately reflects the UDC proceedings.)

Chairman (Typed   Member (Typed Name)   Member (Typed Name)
Name/Signature)

DISCIPLINE HEARING OFFICER REPORT   CDFRM   *206-258*

U.S. DEPARTMENT OF JUSTICE   FEDERAL BUREAU OF PRISONS

INSTITUTION	FCC Terre Haute		INCIDENT REPORT NUMBER			2783086
INMATE NAME	BUCKNER, Bruce		REG NO	20452-075	UNIT	A/F
DATE OF INCIDENT		11.12.2015	DATE OF INCIDENT REPORT			12.15.2015
OFFENSE CODE(S)/CHARGES		104 – Possession of a Weapon 201 – Fighting With Another Person 224 – Assault (Less Serious Injury) 307 – Refusing a Direct Order				

I.	**NOTICE OF CHARGE(S)**						
A.	Advanced written notice of the charge (copy of Incident Report) was given to inmate on:					12.15.2015	
B.	The DHO Hearing was held on:		02.03.2016				
C.	The inmate was advised of his/her rights before the DHO on:		12.28.2015	A copy of the advisement of rights form is attached.			
II.	**STAFF REPRESENTATIVE**						
A.	Inmate declined staff representative.			Yes:	X	No:	
B.	The following staff representative appeared:			N/A			
C.	Requested staff representative declined or could not appear. The inmate was advised he could request the hearing be postponed to obtain another staff representative. The inmate chose to: N/A						
D.	Staff representative		N/A			was appointed.	
E.	Staff representative statement:						
N/A							
III.	**PRESENTATION OF EVIDENCE**						
A.	The inmate	ADMITS		DENIES		NEITHER	X	the charge(s).
B.	Summary of inmate statement:						
Inmate Buckner elected not to make a statement.							
C.	Witness(es):						
1.	The inmate requested witness(es).			Yes		No:	X
2.	The following persons were called as witnesses at the hearing and appeared (Include each witnesses' name, title, register number and statement as appropriate.):						
N/A		#	Statement:				
N/A		#	Statement:				
N/A		#	Statement:				

INMATE COPY

Page 1

102

DISCIPLINE HEARING OFFICER REPORT CDFRM

U.S. DEPARTMENT OF JUSTICE

FEDERAL BUREAU OF PRISONS

inmates were ordered to cease their actions and lay on the ground to which neither inmate complied. Lt. Thompson states that after OC gas was deployed, inmate Mitchell halted his actions, and inmate Buckner struck the officer in the hand in an attempt to knock the OC canister out of his hand.

A supporting memorandum from Lt. Z. Cochran states he responded to a call for assistance in Unit A-2 where he observed the housing unit officer placing inmate Buckner on the ground. Lt. Cochran continues to say that he assisted in controlling inmate Buckner until restraints could be applied.

An Injury Assessment form completed by Nurse T. McDaniel states Officer J. Kremitzki was examined after he was struck in the hand by an inmate when he was attempting to deploy the OC gas.

A photo of Officer J. Kremitzki was taken in order to show him as the victim of an assault.

A Clinical Encounter completed by Nurse T. Haddix was completed for inmate Buckner where he was noted as having a small circle of discoloration on the tip of his tongue.

A Clinical Encounter completed by NR-P C. McGee states inmate Mitchell was found to have sustained a one inch superficial laceration to the posterior scalp.

Photos of inmates Buckner and Mitchell were taken in order to show the injuries they sustained during the incident and to record their involvement in the incident.

Section 11 of the Incident Report describes the actions of inmate Buckner as possessing a weapon, fighting with another inmate, refusing an order and assaulting a staff member. Specifically, inmate Buckner was observed using a broomstick to strike inmate Mitchell. Inmate Mitchell was observed using a chair to strike inmate Buckner. Both inmates were ordered by the reporting officer to cease their actions, however to no avail. The report states inmate Buckner was observed reaching down to pick up a piece of broken broomstick at which time Officer Kremitzki ordered him to drop the weapon and then presented his OC canister. The report continues to say that inmate Buckner then hit Officer Kremitzki's hand in an attempt to knock the gas canister out of his hand. During the hearing, inmate Buckner elected to remain silent. The DHO believes that if inmate Buckner had not committed the prohibited act he would have made a statement and presented a defense to the charges. During the UDC hearing, inmate Buckner stated the "write-up is over five working days." As noted above, inmate Buckner was informed the Incident Report process had been suspended due to the report having to be rewritten and subsequently referred to the AUSA for review in a possible criminal matter. Inmates who possess weapons and engage in physical altercations with staff and inmates are a direct threat to the safety and security of the institution. The DHO also considered inmate Buckner's prior discipline history of guilty findings for Code 201 incidents in order to show a proclivity towards this specific misconduct. This in addition to Section 11 of the Incident Report, supporting memorandums, photos and medical assessment forms are evidence the prohibited act was committed.

Based on the greater weight of the evidence, the DHO finds inmate Buckner committed the prohibited acts of Code 104, Possession of a Weapon, Code 201, Fighting With Another Inmate, Code 224, Assaulting Another Person (Less Serious Injury) and Code 307, Refusing a Direct Order.

VI.	SANCTION OR ACTION TAKEN

Code 104:
41 Days Disallowance of Good Conduct Time
27 Days Forfeit Non-Vested Good Conduct Time
120 Days Commissary Restriction
120 Days Email Restriction

Code 201:
27 Days Disallowance of Good Conduct Time
90 Days Commissary Restriction
90 Days Email Restriction

103

DISCIPLINE HEARING OFFICER REPORT   CDFRM

U.S. DEPARTMENT OF JUSTICE   FEDERAL BUREAU OF PRISONS

3.	The following persons requested were not called for the reason(s) given:							
N/A		#	Statement:					
4.	Unavailable witnesses were asked to submit written statements and those statements received were considered.			Yes		No	N/A	X
D.	Documentary Evidence:							

The inmate did not submit documentary evidence. All evidence used by the DHO is listed in Section V.

E.	Confidential information was used by DHO in support of his findings, but was not revealed to the inmate. The confidential information was documented in a separate report. The confidential information has been (confidential informants have been) determined to be reliable because:
N/A	

IV.	FINDINGS OF THE DHO	
X	A.	The act was committed as charged.
	B.	The following act was committed:
	C.	No prohibited act was committed.

V.   SPECIFIC EVIDENCE RELIED ON TO SUPPORT FINDINGS

Inmate Buckner's due process rights were reviewed by the DHO during the hearing. Inmate Buckner stated he understood his rights, did not submit documentary evidence, and did not request any witnesses. Administrative notice is being given due to inmate Buckner initially requesting the appearance of a staff representative for his hearing. However, on February 3, 2016, inmate Buckner signed a statement requesting to waive his right to the staff representative.

Administrative notice is given due to there being a delay in the delivery of this Incident Report, and the investigation of this Incident Report. Specifically, the Incident Report was rewritten in order to ensure the incident was properly documented in Section 11. Following the rewrite, the Incident Report was suspended pending referral of an inmate criminal matter for investigation on December 15, 2015, and released for administrative processing on December 26, 2015. Inmate Buckner did not provide any evidence this delay hindered his ability to provide a defense.

Administrative Notice is given due to inmate Buckner refusing to sign the Inmate Rights and the Notice of Discipline Hearing forms. Inmate Buckner was advised of his rights and specifically asked if he wanted a staff representative or witness, and declined the same. Inmate Buckner refusal to sign the form was witnessed and noted by Counselor S. Williams.

As stated by Officer J. Kremitzki in the incident report:

On above date and at approximately 5:45pm I S/O J. Kremitzki was returning to the unit from the crossover when I noticed I/m 24254-076 Mitchell, Darnell Fighting with I/m #20452-075 Buckner, Bruce in the unit dayroom. I/m Buckner was using a stick from a broom as a weapon and striking I/m Mitchell with it numerous times in the face and upper body. I/m Mitchell was using a chair and was striking I/m Buckner with it at his upper torso. I called for assistance as I ran over to the inmates and ordered them both to stop fighting and drop the weapon, both inmates refused. I turned to I/m Buckner an observed him reach down to pick up a broken piece of wood from the broom stick. I then gave him an order to drop the weapon as I presented my can of O.C and stated "Get down OC, OC. He then hit my right hand trying to knock my OC canister away from his direction. At this time I administered one (2) second burst of O.C. I then placed inmate Buckner on the floor with the least amount of force necessary and applied mechanical restraints. I/m Buckner was escorted by staff from the housing unit to be medically assessed as the rest of the unit was secured with no further incidents. This is a re-write from 11-12-2015.

A supporting memorandum from Lt. D. Thompson states inmates Buckner and Mitchell were observed striking each other in the common are of the unit with a broom stick and plastic chair respectively. Lt. Thompson continues to say that the

104

DISCIPLINE HEARING OFFICER REPORT   CDFRM

U.S. DEPARTMENT OF JUSTICE   FEDERAL BUREAU OF PRISONS

3.	The following persons requested were not called for the reason(s) given:								
N/A		#	Statement:						
4.	Unavailable witnesses were asked to submit written statements and those statements received were considered.			Yes		No		N/A	X
D	Documentary Evidence:								

The inmate did not submit documentary evidence. All evidence used by the DHO is listed in Section V.

E.	Confidential information was used by DHO in support of his findings, but was not revealed to the inmate. The confidential information was documented in a separate report. The confidential information has been (confidential informants have been) determined to be reliable because:
N/A	

IV.	FINDINGS OF THE DHO	
X	A.	The act was committed as charged.
	B.	The following act was committed:
	C.	No prohibited act was committed.

V.	SPECIFIC EVIDENCE RELIED ON TO SUPPORT FINDINGS

Inmate Buckner's due process rights were reviewed by the DHO during the hearing. Inmate Buckner stated he understood his rights, did not submit documentary evidence, and did not request any witnesses. Administrative notice is being given due to inmate Buckner initially requesting the appearance of a staff representative for his hearing. However, on February 3, 2016, inmate Buckner signed a statement requesting to waive his right to the staff representative.

Administrative notice is given due to there being a delay in the delivery of this Incident Report, and the investigation of this Incident Report. Specifically, the Incident Report was rewritten in order to ensure the incident was properly documented in Section 11. Following the rewrite, the Incident Report was suspended pending referral of an inmate criminal matter for investigation on December 15, 2015, and released for administrative processing on December 26, 2015. Inmate Buckner did not provide any evidence this delay hindered his ability to provide a defense.

Administrative Notice is given due to inmate Buckner refusing to sign the Inmate Rights and the Notice of Discipline Hearing forms. Inmate Buckner was advised of his rights and specifically asked if he wanted a staff representative or witness, and declined the same. Inmate Buckner refusal to sign the form was witnessed and noted by Counselor S. Williams.

As stated by Officer J. Kremitzki in the incident report:

On above date and at approximately 5:45pm I S/O J. Kremitzki was returning to the unit from the crossover when I noticed I/m 24254-076 Mitchell, Darnell Fighting with I/m #20452-075 Buckner, Bruce in the unit dayroom. I/m Buckner was using a stick from a broom as a weapon and striking I/m Mitchell with it numerous times in the face and upper body. I/m Mitchell was using a chair and was striking I/m Buckner with it at his upper torso. I called for assistance as I ran over to the inmates and ordered them both to stop fighting and drop the weapon, both inmates refused. I turned to I/m Buckner an observed him reach down to pick up a broken piece of wood from the broom stick. I then gave him an order to drop the weapon as I presented my can of O.C and stated "Get down OC, OC. He then hit my right hand trying to knock my OC canister away from his direction. At this time I administered one (2) second burst of O.C. I then placed inmate Buckner on the floor with the least amount of force necessary and applied mechanical restraints. I/m Buckner was escorted by staff from the housing unit to be medically assessed as the rest of the unit was secured with no further incidents. This is a re-write from 11-12-2015.

A supporting memorandum from Lt. D. Thompson states inmates Buckner and Mitchell were observed striking each other in the common are of the unit with a broom stick and plastic chair respectively. Lt. Thompson continues to say that the

Sales Invoice ----S.B.U.----
Terre Haute - FCC
USP
Account No. 20452075   TF12213
BUCKNER, BRUCE
03/14/2016 12:27:43 PM TXW6644069   08

BEGINNING BALANCES:
Available Balance is $2,601.70
Spending Limit Balance is $360.00
Account Balance is $2,751.70

Qty   Description   Price

  20 FOREVER $9.80

                   Total $9.80

Charge 20452075 $9.80

Items marked with * are Local Use Only

ENDING BALANCES:
Available Balance is $2,591.90
Spending Limit Balance is $360.00
Account Balance is $2,741.90

Signature

ALL SALES ARE FINAL.

106

Sales Invoice ---S.R.U.---
Terre Haute - FCI
USP
Account No. 20452075   IF12487
BUCKNER, BRUCE
01/11/2016 01:44:13 PM TXN6528824   99

BEGINNING BALANCES:
Available Balance is $2,265.92
Spending Limit Balance is $360.00
Account Balance is $2,315.92

Qty   Description   Price

  1 FOREVER $0.49

                 Total $0.49

Charge 20452075 $0.49

Items marked with $ are Local Use Only

ENDING BALANCES:
Available Balance is $2,265.43
Spending Limit Balance is $360.00
Account Balance is $2,315.43

Signature

ALL SALES ARE FINAL

107

Sales Invoice ---B.B.B.---
Terr Haute - FCC
UNP
Account No. 20432075   TF12481
BUCKNER, BRILE
12/14/2015 07:03:18 AM TXN4401767   38

BEGINNING BALANCES:
Available Balance is $2,777.41
Spending Limit Balance is $410.40
Account Balance is $2,987.41

Qty   Description   Price
                                          $9.00
   20 FOREVER $1.95
    1 DEODORANT, POWER

              Total $11.76

Charge 20432075 $11.76

Items Marked with # are Local Use Only

ENDING BALANCES:
Available Balance is $2,323.76
Spending Limit Balance is $406.05
Account Balance is $2,975.72

Signature

ALL SALES ARE FINAL.

515
200
515   4655 15
       50

The day was January, 28 2016 9:45A.M on a Thursday. When I walk up to the cell door to the Guard. He was screaming "DHO" I thought he might was looking at my name on the list because I had been in the SHU 78 days at this time 30 days waiting on DHO. But he was not screaming to me. I was anxious to know when I will see DHO "Guard" I said "check the list and tell me when DHO will come to see me."

For some reason the man in cell 256 next to me had his window covered up. Having your window cover up in prison is breaking the rules .The guard started screaming into cell 256 for the men in there to uncover the window. One guy walks up to the cell window to uncover it. The guard not knowing someone was in there dead. Ask him to turn around to be handcuff for DHO.

"No!" he said "I killed my celly!" That was his exact words. It was the most grimace voice I have ever heard coming from a cell. The look I seen in the guard eyes I knew that prisoner was not playing in that cell. The guard started rushing trying to look pass the man standing in the way of the body. He said "uncover the body"

He then calls for back up when the other guards came to the cell it was a since of unbelief. They were screaming "TURN AROUND AND CUFF-UP!" At first he was hesitant to cuff up, but he finally gave in. When they open the cell door everybody was looking at him. He had killed his celly last night. All I seen was a blank expression on his face.

The man that walked out of cell 256 I just talk to him a few days early. When he first came on the range I holler at him through the vent. One never knows until one asks. The man might be from the same city or state. So I ask the regular routine question that was ask to me when I came to live in Terre Haute.

One Question I ask was where he was from which he said Oklahoma. The next day he had a seizure so bad that the guards found him stretch out on the floor. He was rush to an outside hospital, but I never seen him come back.

He did not seem weird or nothing like that to me. One thing I noticed from talking to him was that his feet were planted permanently in prison. What I mean by his feet being planted firmly in prison I could tell he had a lot of time to spend in prison. Just so you know he was in his early twenty's.

Back to my testimony it got serious the nurses was in front of the cell asking if the victim needs CPR. "Is he moving?" one guard asks, "No" another guard says. All this talking was happening right outside my cell door. After a few minutes had past the Warden plus a couple more big guys at Terre Haute arrived.

The Warden gave the permission for cell 256 to be open. A lady walks in with a camera. Then all I could see was flashes coming out the cell. "Who is he" a guard asks that walked on the range. This guy a few cells down yells "Baby Ock!"

One of them hospital stretchers was place outside the cell with a blue body bag placed on top of it I was in cell 257 right next door so I could see everything. And hear everything. It was other prisoners on the range screaming out "IF THE GUARD WAS DOING HIS JOB BABY OCK WOULD NOT BE DEAD!" "BABY OCK SAID HE DID NOT WANT TO BE IN THAT CELL." He was really making the guard that was worker the range look bad in front of the Warden and the other big guys at Terre Haute.

This guy from Texas was yelling "WHEN YOU ALL GONE GET THAT BODY OUT OF THERE?" The guards did not respond to him. All of them just kept on doing the job at hand.

One guard walks out of cell 256 in a state of shock. He stood in front of my cell explaining to another guard what he had just seen. He stated that the dead victim had a long cut on his forehead. He also had a cut throat. The guard was animated when speaking on what had caused the dead of Baby Ock.

Finally the body bag was taken into the cell, but the body was not place in the bag. Baby Ock was place inside a prison blanket with one thrown over him. When he was rolled out of the cell I was looking at his feet hanging out the end of the blanket. He was stiff as a board rolling out the unit.

The range was quit for a few minutes after all the medical staff, guards, and the warden left. Everybody was thinking about what had happen to Baby Ock the last few nights he was alive I know me and my cellmate was. He was speaking on what could drive the killer to do something like that to the young boy.

Note: While doing time in prison it is a lot of demons that will possess your mind body, and soul. It will not be you just going to a prison doing your prison term then go home. Not the case at all. Being in them cells for years will fill your body

113

with poison. Fill your mind, body, and soul with unwanted thoughts. So ask yourself do I want to experience poison filling my body? Do I want to hang myself? Do I want to die in a cell? NO! You know what you need to do Think, Think and, Think of an idea. That will cause my life go in a positive place.

The guard on duty was walking around checking the cells every 15 minutes. Making sure a change of reaction did not start because everyone was paranoid. He did not want the whole range to start killing their cellmates or worst a killing spree. Did he think everyone was thinking about killing their cell mate?

If he did the guard was right because I was definitely thinking about killing the man in my cell I was not gone end up getting taken out of Terre Haute in a body bag.

Some of the inmates stop the guard to ask him. "When are they gone come to ask question?" My cellmate was one of them guys. He wanted to use what had happen to his advantage. Giving false information to get him ship to where he wanted to be. He was a check in from the compound I do not know way he was allowed to be in the cell with me because I was a max inmate.

After a few hours had past the forensic workers came to examining the crime scene. It was a cart by my cell that had stacks of small plastic suitcases on top of it. The forensic workers would grab one then walk in the cell. All I was thinking she in there doing scientific testing with techniques trying to find out exactly how the prisoner was killed.

January 28 is a day I will never forget. All the stories I heard about living life in prison. Was no lie some people do not make it out of prison. At any time your life could be taking from you. One day you are here the next day gone. Prison is not a cool place. Think about where you want your future to go before you do something stupid.

The next morning everybody was still shock about what had happen in cell 256. All on the range conversation was going on about how the killer tricked Baby Ock to come in the cell with him. That he was wrong for doing that young boy like that. What possess him to cut his face up?

The SIS people came on the range pulling everybody out the cell early for the investigation on the murder of Baby Ock. "Buckner is you ready to answer some question?" A guard screams threw the cell door. "Yeah come on" I got up to be handcuff. The way it went in the SHU if the door was gone be open. Both men have to be in handcuff. This was the first time the cell was open while he was in the cell. He thought he did not have to cuff-up." You got to cuff-up too" I said to him. So he jumps off the top bunk to be cuff.

Everybody that was planning on using what happen last night as an advantage was yelling out the door I mean it was loud. Walking down the range a Caucasian said "Bruce you all right?" "Yeah way wouldn't I be!"

We were placed in an old holding cell with the bars I stretch the old bars look because I want you to get the picture how ugly prison is. It is not good for a man mind to be behind something like bars. It will do something to your mind if you're not strong enough to hold as a man.

My cellmate said "Bruce will you say that you heard me talking to the guy in cell 256 last night for a few hours. "No I am not about to do something like that." "It will not help you.

A pretty SIS lady I have never seen on the compound pulls my cellmate out the cell first to be question.

The other pretty red head SIS lady came to get me. While I was sitting in the chair I thought about helping my celly get shipped to another prison, but no I finally said to myself.

All the answers I gave to the SIS were the truth. She ask did I hear any screaming, kicking on the door. The answer to that question was no. All was said and done with. While I was walking back to my cell .The guards had all types of food laid out on the table. When I tell you that food was looking tasty to me it was the truth.

Back in the cell we pulls out the chess board to play a few games of chess. While talking about how the investigation went with the SIS. The games lasted a few hours as always. We always played a lot of games to past time.

After all the chess games I got back on my bunk to read a few magazines I had bought from a guy on the range. It was one I really like the Sub-Zero magazine the reason being in Tennessee Sub-Zero was not a magazine that was in the prisons, but if the prisoners only knew what kind of girls was in it. Plus the questions the interviewer asks. It will become popular. It was also a XXL in my collection. It was not as freaky, but the XXL magazine will do. Now the Straight Stunning that magazine is hot too. After reading every word in the magazines the day went by fairly smooth.

The follower day I got on my exercising. First sets I warm up by doing 10 push every 2 minutes. After feeling my muscles had warmed up my real sets begun. First Navy Seals, if you do not know what a Navy Seal exercise is. It goes like this first you got to be in a stance position. You drop down to a push up stand. Kick one leg to your chest. Do a push-up; kick the other leg to your chest. Do a push.

When I am all done with my first exercise my reps add up to 100 plus. The next exercise is push-ups which is my favorite exercise. One could never do too many push-ups I have done thousands of them. Doing push-ups is an exercise that a prisoner like me do to stay fit at all times. Plus it helps relieve oneself from stressing.

Another muscle I work is my back arms I get at the end of my bunk and do the exercise that way. Doing back arms are very easy to do in the cell. One does not need a lot of space. At the end of my back arm exercise I done 20 sets at 70 reps add that up to see how hard I was going.

My next exercise which is the last one sit -ups. Now this exercise takes a lot of work to get results. The reason being for me I eat a lot. Sit-ups are tough I only do 20 at a time when I am finish all together 100 reps. When I finish my exercising routine I press my bunk by reading a book.

At this time I was reading a good book. It really had me at another level. The name of the book was "Light Up Your Child's Mind". Yeah I was on my way out. Reading "Light Up Your Child Mind" was a goal that I set for myself to do for my daughters I been out of there life a long time. I needed to put in extra work to be a better father to the two.

This morning was January 31 in the middle of the night I had woke up because I could not sleep. The nightmare I had was too bad. The number 14 was pressing on my chest real hard pressuring me to kill my cellmate. I was telling myself I am not the number 14. You will not get the best of me; I need to get home to my daughters. It was a Bible next to my bunk that I picked up to read. The chapter of choice was psalm 23. This will not be the last time the Bible got me through a horrible thought.

After realizing what time it was I pick up my radio waiting on one of my favorite shows to come on. It was a long wait too. A few hours had pass before my show actually came on. At 5:00A.M. Ryan Seacrest was on my radio "American top 40 hits." On this Sunday Charlie Puth was hosting the show... His new album had come out Friday. So he was doing the show promoting his body of work. He was doing a real good job too. Every Sunday I listen to Ryan Seacrest morning show even though I was in Terre Haute Federal Prison. Listening to Ryan Seacrest was a good Sunday.

When the show goes off breakfast be at the cell door. This Sunday morning brown cereal with fruit in a cup was on the tray. Not much to eat just enough to get to the next tray I went back to sleep after eating. Hoping I did not have a nightmare. A nightmare is prison is the worst. For example one night I had a dream I was choking a ghost. The ghost had my hand in his mouth trying to bite it off. My hand really started hurting so I woke up. When I look at my hand it was bleeding. True testimony I even talk to this lady Ms. Adams about the dream when she came down the range.

Anyway I went back to sleep Woke back up at 12:45P.M to wipe myself off from a wet dream. Now having a wet dream is the best dream to have in prison. Man having one of them is like the lieutenant saying pack your stuff Bruce you are going home. The bad thing about the dream is it only happen every blue moon.

At 1:00P.M brunch was at the door... When I took a seat on my bunk to eat what was on the tray. It was Pancakes, eggs, potatoes, some pink, white looking meat and slices of green Cantaloupe. For some reason the food was cold. The guard working the range probable had the trays out there just sitting getting cold before he decided to pass the trays out. Stuff like that goes on when the guards want to fuck with the range, but that is not even close to the spiteful stuff that the guards do in Terre Haute.

Another day gone while in Terra Haute I went to sleep for the night at 10:10P.M I wanted to have another wet dream this night. Yeah sometimes I try to force a wet dream out of my head

It was now Monday February 1, I forgot what time I woke up this morning. Usually I would have look at the time on my radio but did not. This morning was country breakfast biscuits with gravy, oatmeal, and potatoes. Which was not cook well, and an apple that is almost always rotten. By the tray being cold made it horrible eating it.

After washing my hands my cellmate ask me to play chess. First I had to think about because loosing be making me mad. He know I be feeling like going up side his head when I loss. In my pass I have smack a man for winning too many games playing me, but I have learn how to control my anger a little better.

Plus it passes time that I really want to pass. For some reason I be feeling like I am playing myself when we got the chess board out. It is like he is hiding from me. By not showing his real self so I could catch his next move. He could play all day like that which it made me mad at the world I had to leave the board to read my books. .

At the time I was writing the words of this book I was looking at the time. It was 10:20P.M. It is 49 minutes pass the time I would be in the bed trying to go to sleep. By being in prison so long I like getting in bed at the same time going to sleep every night for no apparent reason.

Me being a prisoner waking up in a cell doing the time at hand, and doing the same stuff every day which will get me nowhere in life was starting to make me feel hopeless. Not so hopeless that I will kill myself. Just feeling so bad about what I was going through in my life. My life had an F as a grade in Terre Haute.

The only thing that was hope to me at the time I was going through the harsh experience in this book. Was if some mail came through the cell door for me. Mail calling time really made my day. I always wanted to see what is going on with the family. Read how life was treating others. Note: One time my mother told me my lil cousin was having a baby

Some guys been in prison so long worry about mail is an understatement. The only worries on these guys mind are If the trays are hot enough coming through the flap, are the guards following the rules that they are supposed to follow, and writing a BP8(also known as) grievance form on the guard if he or she broke a rule Not forget starting confusing

This guard walks down the range his name is Red . He told some guy to "pack his stuff you are moving down stairs. The guy said "way" then Red said "because you have been talking to the other guy on the other side of the vent. "No I have not, I do not know him." "Still pack your stuff you are moving down stairs to a new cell." "Red I am not moving anywhere!" "You all saw what happen the other day in cell 256 I got family that loves me out there." He was scared.

Everyone was still shock about what had happen January 28. No one wants to move with a new cellmate that he did not know. The new guy might have a knife or some other tool he could use to hurt his new cell partner. The new guy might have that tempter that will make him snap in the middle of the night like me.

Like I said before I was move to USP Terre Haute I was across the street. With lower points, but my points went up for fighting, drinking. Over there was worst of the worst Cartel members, Avenues members I have been around all types of men, but Living in USP Terre every prisoner in not a real man. One never knows what type of prisoner in the cell. So I really did not blame him.

The man that killed Baby Ock was crazy. The guard put the word on the range about what happen in the cell. He carved a cross onto the dead guy forehead. In the middle of his chest he carved Satan. From my point of view no one will really know what happen in cell 256 that night, but one person the killer

The guard that put that word on the range also looks the killer information up. The reason he was in prison he killed a cab driver then drove the car somewhere. Found a place to leave the car, but not before sitting the car on fire.

This guy yelled out to the guard on the range "Baby Ock was gay. It was wrong on the unit manager for putting him in the cell with a man that was not gay". See this goes back to what type of stuff the guard be doing. By them putting him in a cell with a straight man put is life in danger. Real men do not want to live around gay men.

Diamond: If you do not want to be in a cell with a punk that suck dick. Or a man that like to fuck punks. STAY OUT OF PRISON! Do what is right by the law. It will eventually work out in the long run. Plus with an education or trade either one will work wonders in your future.

Well me I had to learn the hard way. Right now I am 5 years 9 months in prison the reason I am writing this telling my story. Being a man of God deep in my spiritual being do not want any other human being to experience living life in a prison cell if I could help it. Really I hope that this book will put a picture in your teenage head or your adult head that living in the streets. Doing stuff in the dark that will put you in a cell if you are caught is not good. Grow up learn from my mistakes it will make you smart.

Plus it will be gangsta.

This is how I feel about prison now. It should be a class in school that teaches students about prison life. Have real prisoners or men that have been to prison to talk real to the students I believe it will help society out. If not that make every student read a book about prison life. So the book can put fear in the students. This way the youth will be scared to commit any crimes.

That will be a good course in school some of the school killings that are going on in America will stop. Sincerely some fear need to be put in these growing up teenagers today because once a human experience living life in prison. Better yet hearing about a Federal Prison a smart human will change, so again fear need to be put in the youth heart at a very young age Fear, Fear, and more Fear of going to prison.

Knowing in prison he or she will be around all different nationality of people. Seeing open gay man or women talk about having sex with different partners. It is the most disturbing thing ever. Really I have never seen or heard of a gay Indian, Mexican before in my life until I came to Terre Haute. Please believe me when I tell you this I have nothing against gay people. It is just something I do not want to be around a long period of time.

You will not either if you was in prison. That type of thinking does not need to rub off on straight people. Being around gays will have you thinking in way you have never thought before. Your mind will really play tricks on you if you are not a person of God. Living in a prison cell will have you thinking it is alright in God eyes to like the same sex.

"Buckner get ready for DHO" the guard yelled through the door. "Yeah I am ready" I really was not I was exercising doing my daily Navy Seals. It was a shot policy I had under my bed too I wanted to show DHO to get my shot dismissed. The shot that I am having a hearing on was for Assault Any Person, Possession of Weapon, Fighting with another Person, and Refusing to Obey Orders of Staff.

Second shot Assault Any Person. Even if I am guilty the policy I put in my back pocket. States that unity team had 5 working days to UDC me on the incident report. (Meaning having a hearing to see if I was gone plead guilty, or not guilty for the charges)

Walking down the stairs I saw the nice looking woman guard that work the compound I like also the nice looking psychology lady. The reason I am telling you about the two women I saw. Please believe me everything in prison is ugly. Not the people, but the whole living environment in the SHU. Getting to look at a pretty woman every once in a while relax my mind.

Diamond: If you love to be in love STAY AWAY FROM CRIME! Please find something positive to do with your life a jewel to put in your head.

Back to the ugly part. Now at this moment I am sitting in a chair in the DHO office. "Where are you from Buckner?" The hearing officer ask "I am from Nashville, TN" Nashville Tennessee the hearing officer repeated. "Yeah" I said to the officer. My mind was thinking in a very high frequency. "So I said to him trying to be the bigger man "I take full responsibility for my action on my shot."

"But my unit team did not come UDC me within 5 working days." Man I need to get this shot dismissed I was thinking. Every prisoner that then had a shot before knows the date is important. Every detail supposed to be right. Reaching in my back pocket I pulled out the policy. He took a close look at the policy that I had handed him. He then pulls out a different shot that he had in a folder in front of him. Then he would look at the shots. We went back and forth about the dates on my shot. It was the same shot, but different dates. The guard had written the shot over making it look like I was UDC within 5 working days I was mad because that was not correct I had to fight we went back & fourth again, but I could notice this was a no win for me.

Something else you need to know about prison. A prisoner is never right in an officer eye. If a man or woman ends up in prison there rights are taken away from them. It is really no help for the prisoner. All the prisoner can do is take what he or she got coming like an adult.

Diamond: Find something in life that you enjoy doing that is legal. If you enjoy what you are doing it is the key to not working. It will feel more like a hobby.

Please do not end up in a place like Terre Haute life will be over with has you know it.

Back to my hearing the DHO officer hit me hard on each count that is on my shot Me being the man I am was not new to this I brushed it off my shoulders like Jay Z rapped in his song ,and I took what he gave me like a man. All ways remember this before you do something that is not right. Once you are in trouble it is very hard getting out of that trouble. The problems that come with crime are not worth the amount of time that will be taking out of your life. And another diamond the negative guys or females you are hanging around you need to stay away from them people even if they are family members.

Being a positive human being is cool. Doing the right thing in life is cool. Being around up lifting people is cool. Living life on a positive term will pay off in the future. Smart is the new way to achieve life in abundance.

After getting done with DHO I could see freedom again. In the following week my unit team should be to my cell door. Speaking to me about my half way house date I was relax a little about the upcoming days. While thinking well about my outcome grabbed me radio to turn on my afternoon show. It was exactly 2:00P.M the time Dr. Anderson show comes on Station 91.9 the Catholic station.

Dr. Anderson is a man that is full of life, knowledge, and wisdom. He is a very uplifting human being I think highly of Dr. Anderson even though I never meet him. Listening to him one day you will really enjoy that hour listening he speaks to people all over the world.

Listening to Dr. Anderson or better yet the Catholic station period is a great way to pass time in prison or to listening to while in the free world. It is so much knowledge that the Catholics give. The faith was very strong to me. The people are wonderful. Go listening to the station.

On this morning February 4 I woke up to a not so healthy breakfast. The tray had grits with a slice of cake on the side. Living life in prison is the only place I know that serve cake for breakfast. If you know a place serve cake for breakfast contact me please.

After breakfast I did not go back to sleep. The guard asks me did I want to go see the dentist. "Yeah I do" before I handcuff I had to brush my teeth for the dentist. The guard walks off . A few minutes went pass I heard the guard walking back down the range. "Are you ready now Buckner" the guard said to me.

I did not say nothing I just walked to the door to be cuff .When the cell door open I was search, and a chain was placed around my waist like they was driving me to an outside dentist. "Where are we going" I ask the guard "Just upstairs" he said back. "Okay for the way the chains are on me I thought we were leaving the premises. This something the transportation does when an inmate is taken outside the premises. We walked down where the DHO officer did my hearing.

It was a hallway that we walk down to get on an elevator. When I got up where the dentist office was located. To the left of me were units that were identical to how the units look where I was living. The only difference was that death row prisoners were living in these units. One particular Death Row prisoner you should know about. He goes by The Boston Bomber

I was place in a holding cell. Then 5 more inmates was place in the cell with me. It was another inmate that could not be place in the cell because the cell was too small. He was place somewhere else.

Inside the holding cell was I another African American, Puerto Rican, a Mexican. All of us came from different areas of the SHU.

The Mexican the guy sitting next to me started having a connection about how to put a BP8 on the guards. Just so you are not confuse a BP8 is a form that is filled out on a guard that have broken a rule. I and this guy sitting beside me stood up to look out the holding cell because we heard people walking in our direction. It was the dentist with two ladies. "Take a seat!" The dentist said. He could see that we were looking at the women to hard.

The guy next to me said something back to the dentist. Whatever he said had the dentist up set. He came out his office to confront the person who he thought said something .Which was me "Your appointment as been canceled!" "It was not me" I said fighting back. The dentist did not believe me. The guard walks up from hearing the commotion. The dentist said "the prisoner sitting in the chair in the right corner appointment as been canceled!"

The guard knew me from across the street. Deep down he knew I was not the type of prisoner that fight with staff. The guy that really said what the dentist heard finally stood up. "It was me that said something when you walked off." "No it was not you!" "It was him!" The dentist said. The dentist still had a chip on his shoulder. The dentist stated that he will send both of us back to hour cells.

"No it was not him it was me." The guard walks in the office with the dentist. "Do not jump on me I am not gone let you take the fall for what I said" The guard walks out the dentist office toward the holding cell where we was. He asks the guy to turn around and cuff up? It did not go as easy as he the guard thought it should have. The African American guy was not going back to his cell that easy. He was a trouble maker. "No I had been waiting for two months to get this tooth pull." "Plus I did not do nothing wrong" he said. "The dentist told us to sit down." "My precise words were way do we have to sit down?" He explains to the guard. He went on to say "this is a free country we have the freedom of speech!"

"You still need to turn around with your hands around your back to cuff up." "No go get the lieutenant." He said not backing down. The guard walks off like he was going to get the lieutenant, but that was not the case. He came back with three built guards. Everyone already knew what they came to do. The situation was getting ugly. He asks him again to cuff up. "No I know my rights" he said.

The guard said "you either gone walk out like a man or get carry out like a Bitch!" The guy still did not budge. The cell was open. "You three come with me" the guard said. We all walks out to be place in another cell. Well not a cell but the death row visitation room.

"What is your name" the Mexican asks me. "Bruce" I said back to the Mexican. "Bruce you handle that like a man." "I appreciate you saying that" If it was not for man's speaking up the dentist would have most definitely sent me back. A few minutes past before the guard comes back to get us out of the Death Row visitation area. The other guy was gone back to the unit.

See the guards will always win. Prison is not made for inmates to overpower the guards. Even if the numbers was even.

At the end the day guards will win the fight. Never fight the guards. Once you step over that boundary it is written in the compute. The guards will have a chip on their shoulder every time your name comes up. They will make your time harder then what you want to deal with.

For example you will be on the other side of the United States. Thinking what you did was forgiving or forgot about. Not! Now you are in a new place where the guards already have a chip on their shoulder about you. But you in a peaceful mind set. Then they start chaos.

Another example you might need something important done that the guards have to help you with. He says no to you then just walks away. How will that make you feel?

The dentist calls out my name to come into the office, I took a seat in the chair. Really I did not need to see the dentist. The sick- call I filled out and turned end was two months ago. The only reason I fill one out was to get out the cell. So I was worried about the dentist finding out I was wasting his time.

"Mr. Dentist I do not need my tooth pulled. Just check them out to make sure they are in great condition for me." The dentist did exactly that. Come to find out my gums was infect. "In a few days the nurse will bring you some ibuprofen" he said. My appointment was over with before 3:30 I was back in my cell.

Thursday went by fast it was not any commotion in the unit. This was a good thing. Days like Thursday happens every blue moon too. Plus I and my celly were getting alone.

Friday I did not write in my book. Yes the book you are reading I was writing as the events happen. Each day I would write down stuff that caught my eyes that was interesting. Or I thought someone might need to know what is going on in prison walls.

Saturday I woke up from hearing the guard holler CHOW TIME down the range. This morning we had brown flakes, apple, and cake. The apple was cut in half which I hate because it is brown once it gets through the door I stayed up after eating because of the dream I had. It was one of them mornings again. Where I felt like thinking about the pleasure of the dream. It was my way of feeling, thinking outside of Terre Haute.

To the people that I want this book to help. Take what I am about to say to heart. If you do what is right by the law. Plus take time to deeply meditate getting your thoughts together. A dream will come to you from God. He will tell you exactly what to do. Dreams come true

The things you truly want will be handed to you. Do not get me wrong you will have to jump. Take the leap of faith. The jump could be changing the people that have no value in your future. The way you eat. Once you take the leap of faith. Your dream will come true.

But you also have to work hard for it. Steve Harvey said a person will still experience bumps and bruises from the cliff that you had faith to jump off of. Then your parachute will open. Then you will glide through the air.

President Barack Obama also said working hard will pay off. Personally I believe what Steve Harvey, President Barack Obama said for instance if you are reading this book my hard work paid off. The dreams God was giving me I am now living. It will happen to you once you stop living the life that is not meant for you...

The words in this book are for help. Giving you wisdom, knowledge in areas where you do not have.

If you are reading these words and just brushing them off PLEASE THINK AGAIN. Think about where you really want to be in the future. If you want change you either gone end up in prison with monsters, or DEAD. Because living in the streets is not good. In time you will do something that the judge will put you in prison for. Or you gone do something that's gone get you killed.

Get yourself together even if it mean being along because if you end up living in a prison. You will really experience what being alone is about. Plus with enemies all around you that want to cut your life short.

To all of my readers that have read this book. Spread the word about Living Life in Terre Haute. This book needs to be in every trouble teenagers in the world. Every trouble man in the world, every trouble girl in the world, and every trouble woman in the world. They need to know that prison is a terrible place to live.

Even if you are not a trouble mind I hope this book will help you too. Give you strength to pursuit what will make you happy. Give you drive to see things out. Talk uplifting to a person that needs motivation.

Back to Living life in Terre Haute It was February 10. The day a guard on duty knocks on the cell door. "Tyler get ready for your interview" I was still in bed sleepy, but I had to get up out of bed to be handcuff because of the guard safety. Plus it was part of doing the SHU program.

By the guard asking for just for Tyler I was thinking I could get back in bed. For some much needed rest. That was not the case.

The guard wants me to answer some question too. "Man I am not going" I said still sleepy. Buckner you are already handcuffing. It will only take a few minutes." It would have been the waste of time fighting the guard. Me knowing he does not care how early it was. "Buckner just talk to the people so you will be out the cell for a few minutes." "Do not sleep your time away."

He was fucking with me. He knew both of us were on the paper anyway. Again walking where the interview was to be the nice looking lady I seen the first time was standing to the right of me just standing there doing nothing. A few steps I was back in the same interview room as before. It was not the redhead SIS lady as before, but a man and female from the regional. Yeah those were the big people. The pinstripes suit wearing people. The impression the two showed was serious.

The same questions were asked to me. And I gave the two the same truthful answers as before. It all ended in no time. The one particular guard that was at the door when the killer said he killed his celly. Hand me by my arm walking up the stairs. He sparks a conversation with me about the killer he said, "Dude, criminal history was bad."

This morning was February 12; a good morning I stayed up until my show came on, "Catholics EWTN." A commercial came on with the Pope speaking. He said a beautiful quote, something like, "Get closer to our spiritual identity." That is very so much true. If people would do that, the world will be so much better. The thought of the Pope speaking I had to turn up my radio to get some more spiritual growth or food for the spirit.

The guy talking now is speaking on peace. Something else I really need in my life. Peace of mind. To the troubled minds out there, "You have a talent that God gave, you, brother/sister. The reason you have not found it, is because of your attitude. Your bad attitude is blinding you of your gift. I am for sure you have a bad attitude, Right?

If you answer yes, that is the first thing you need to change. And do not think your personality will change. But your life will change for the better. I am saying change the negative to a positive. Think positive every day. Be more thoughtful about your future. Eventually, things will work out for the better. That is how life will happen. Believe in the power of thinking positive every day.

If a person stays away from the wrong people and places, this is the key. Stay away from the places that will bring out the worst. Go to a library to fill that kind of energy. Then check out a good book. What you need to know is the library can get any book you like. Living Life in Terre Haute I found all types of books to read. Like Sam Walton "Made in America" the man that built all the Walmart's, Donald Trump "The Art of the deal", and Donald Trump "Think Like A Billionaire."

It won't be just you reading. It will be a real enjoyment to you. Note: When you decide to go to the library and start checking books out. You must know the author plus the name of the book. One more thing, know the subject you want to read up on. For example, if you have dreams of building a great business, read the Sam Walton book. If you want to think like a billionaire, Donald Trump is the man to read and study. These are great books I read in Terre Haute. Again going to the library is a real peace of mind.

To the fellas, you might find a nice female there. Again, this book is meant to guide troubled minds in the right direction. It is many activities that are out there made to better us. Sometimes it is who you know that can put you in a better position, but he or she won't if you are still hanging in hazardous environments. So you do your part. Put some real work in. Real work will get noticed.

Clock in every chance you get. It will pay off. Hard work will also give a man or woman a since of value within himself. Also find a real purpose in life that is the key to living life in abundance. If you find logic in the mind, learn to reason with people. Do not show negative attitude if something does not go your way.

Reason with the person because if the path you are on puts you in prison, it will be a whole lot of situations that you are going to reason on. So take what you are reading in this book to heart. Do not make mistakes that will put you in prison. Make adjustments to your life so that you can live a long peaceful and fulfilling life. It want happen right when you want it, but do not worry practice the good behavior. Take small steps like not using bad words. Then once you've had enough practice. The good behavior will just flow out of you. On top of that once you have got yourself together teach the power of thinking positive to others.

Saturday 13 it was 11:19 P.M.

Just got finished playing chess I had to play a few games to pass time. Now that the chess board is put away I am sitting on my bunk thinking about my freedom. How it is not coming fast enough I got 85 days left to live in Terre Haute. These days need to hurry up and pass. Man I am ready to go Plus I am thinking how my life will benefit my daughter's life.

Sunday 14 6:52A.M woke up with a lot on my mind again had a dream with Minster Louis Farrakhan in it. Really had me thinking what God is telling me. Way would I be dreaming about Minster Farrakhan? Was God speaking to me through him? Was I put on Earth to spread the word? It was so many questions I was asking God.

I and Minster Louis Farrakhan were in a race on some type of racing device. All my family was in it. Even my Granny that had been dead for years was in it. She was sitting in the back seat. Right behind me in my ear. We were looking for my Uncle Pac Man. I spotted him walking through a cut the way we enter into the Duplexes from Haynes Garden where my family is from. The dream ended with me and Minister Louis Farrakhan at a finish line.

Dreams are something that happens a lot in prison or me. Some of my best dreams in my life were in prison I mean the dreams where so powerful with so much meaning.

Another dream I had was me living in a mansion more than enough wealth to go around. It was so real to me. In front of the mansion was a water fountain with nothing but quarters in it. Every time a visit came to the house. The loose quarters that was in there pocket was through into the fountain.

Some of the visitor spoke on making a wish. After the quarters was in the fountain. When I count the quarters I was always tens of thousands of dollars in the fountain. The quarter was donated to the poor.

See that is how living in Terre Haute did. The prison was tricking my brain. Had me thinking about all the great stuff I could have been doing with my life, if I only was pursuing something great that gave me purpose in life. Not out in the streets breaking laws.

God put in me to write this book to reach others that are on the wrong path. He put me in prison to talk to me personally. God had to sit me down for a minute because I was not listing to him in the streets breaking the law. Now that I know he has spoken to me. My spirit is filling with joy because God is my Father. Whatever I ask in Jesus name I will receive.

So make sure you pay attention to the dreams you are having. That is a way that God is speaking to you. While you are in the streets breaking the law. You are not gone hear him because it is too much none sense. That has your attention in the streets. Chase your dreams in the free world. Once you are in prison your dream are being wasted. It is not a good feeling. So again pay attention to your dreams so that you can live them.

Now it is exactly 7:00P.M just had a long talk with Tyler. We was talking about how it is in different cities around

America, The population numbers and how that number could be turn into buying customers. What kind of business will be good in each city?

Also having a positive conversation helps the day go smoothly. These kinds of days lower my blood pressure a little bit. Positive conversation does not happen in a place like Terre Haute. The reason being it is a Death Row building. Everyone wants to be the baddest.

Monday 15 Presidents Day I woke up feeling good about my days living in Terre haute getting short. Got 18 days to my freedom I am on my best behavior. It is hard for me, but practice on my behavior for the free world while in prison. My behavior will be perfect in the free world.

Being so close to being home is a great feeling I just had to say that again. All I have to do is chill and lay back. Stay away from shots, and soon I will be home. The rest of the day went by smooth, but rough at the same time. Tyler and I played a few games of chess again. True testimony I get mad every time I loose. That is the rough part of my days. Chess get so competitive we did not go to sleep until 2:00A.M

At 4:00A.M I woke back up my body felt like I been lifting weight. My body was aching it was no use of me going back to sleep. It was not gone happen. All I knew to do was pick up my book to read all the way to breakfast time. When the trays where on the range the guy next door was on one. The tray the guard wanting to give him he did not want it. "Well I will serve you the last tray" the guard said.

"No I am not gone take it!" "You want be eating a meal" the guard said back. "If you do not give me a tray I am popping the sprinkler" the prisoner said back. Next thing I hear was water running. "He did it, pop the sprinkler" Tyler said. This guard walks to his door that I have never seen before on the range. He asks him to turn around with his hands behind his back. And put his hand in the flap to be handcuff. I walks to the door to see what was going on at his cell. It was water all over the range.

Three guards were pushing some of the water to the drain. A lot of the water was also running in some of the cells down the range. Not too much water ran in the cell me and Tyler was in. Usually when someone pops a sprinkler the cells closes to the water gets it. One would have to put blankets in front of the door. We did not have to do that. Some of the other guys on the range did.

After the water was clean up the guys that had wasted a blanket. Wanted theirs to be replace, but the guard said it was not any clean.

The reason the guards was hard on the guy next door he would not take a new cellmate. After his cellmate had left. The guards then wanted to move him to another range. He said he was not going anywhere. He took the cell hostage no one was getting in. Plus he was not coming out.

The guards got all the power. I than been through what this guy next door was doing. To me it is a waste of time and energy at the age I'm at. At the end of the day, week, and years I will need the guard for something. Whatever I might need it will be in the guard job description to do it. He might be nosy and look at my prison history see that I been hard on other guards.

On the other had of giving him a hard time while he is doing his job He will blame you for wasting his time. Then any time one of use needs something done. He will have a grudge and for him helping will be out the picture. Knowing we cannot handle our own business because we are lock behind door.

Friday woke up late. Had a weird dream, but cannot remember enough to tell you the details about what happen. So I'm gone leave this dream alone.

The weekend was okay beside somebody else flooding the cell. This time it was the guy next door. It was water everywhere in my cell had to put blankets on the floor this time. It really was not too bad I learn to take in good from the bad. All I decided to do was use the water that flooded my cell mix some soap with it and mop my floor.

Monday came around with another situation happening, come to find out at wreck. A punk which some prisoner looks at as a girl is a man that like dick. The punk got a knife from another homosexual inmate that was fucking him. The prisoner that was giving the dick wanted the punk to prove his love to him. Then order for him to stick the other homosexual man. So the punk run up on the boyfriend and sticks him in the face. It is some unbelievable moments living in prison. I just could not believe men were acting like this. A man catching a domestic violence charge on another supposed to be man. .

Like two days went pass before the dude that is the man in the relationship get another sex partner. He was the DC prisoner that kept on gossiping with my first celly when I came to the SHU. Come to find out he was a punk that like to take dick up the ass and mouth. He heard that the two

141

homosexual men got into a fight. Then he starts popping sprinklers, throwing trays out of the flap, and refusing other prisoners to move into the cell. Just so he will be put in the cell with the supposed to be man in the relationship.

Living life in Terra Haute homosexuality was a life style.

If a man is not gay he was an outcast to the guards. That is how the guards made us feel whenever I would ask the guards to do something the answer was no. When a homosexual ask the guards to do something they would jump right on it. The homosexuals always got there way. It was not normal or right in my eyes me being a straight man was getting treated terribly by the guards. Terre Haute was a terrible place to live I tell you!

I am a man loving the way a woman moan. Some nights was woken up in the middle of the night from hearing a homosexual moaning loud. A couple doors down the range. It was the most disgusting sound I have ever heard in my life. Just think if you heard a man making noise like a woman makes doing having sex because it feel good. Not right huh? Stay away from crime then!

This morning I was woke up by someone calling my name. The night before I got on him for that damn moaning I heard. That had me mad that I had to hear that. The faggots were calling me out for rack. At first I was gone go out to fight to prove a point. That they had no fight toward a real man like me I wanted to beat the gay out of the two faggots. It was getting to me because the gays were acting like they were real man calling out the real men on the range. Me not worry about losing a fight almost went out to rack. If it was not for my celly telling me not to go because of my half way house date coming up soon. It was also funny so I just laughed the calling out off.

Terre Haute was a terrible place to live again I thought. The homosexuals' had a gang of their own. They had a name for it.

Being in Terre Haute or any prison is a battle between good & evil. It is an ongoing battle in a man head. Because what was once in a man head, heart, and soul is getting pulled out thrown in a cell, and fucked. Then by that happening to the man pushes him to get in a physical fight with every prisoner. Prison gets a man out of tune with reality. All they are force to learn is how to live in a prison lock in a cell.

What I am saying a man got to protect his mind and heart at all times in the free world because the devil presence really exist in the world. He will possess the two organs if the human is not strong enough. God was with me doing all the time I have done. God allow me to control my heart & brain I always pray for strength, wisdom, and knowledge. Sometimes I would see myself killing my cellmate like really it would be blood all over me. God gave me strength not to take action.

He would speak to me telling me Bruce do what is right. Get home to the people that love you. These guys are not worth losing your whole life. Do not let the devil win. My ears were open and were listing.

Diamond: To you, listen, learn and grow.

The following morning me & Tyler was woke up by someone down the range kicking on the door. Plus some yells. The guard was doing rack. He skip someone cell the guy who cell he skip was mad because he was not getting his rack. The guard might have been in a fuck up mood this morning, and

143

did not want to pull all the guys out for rack. It could be a whole list of reasons.

Like having problems at home with the wife or did not get a lot of hours this week. By him getting under the guy skin is making his day a lot better.

Problems every other day. That is how it is living life in Terre Haute or any other prison. It is always something happening or about to happen in prison.

Waking up in a place where one has to look over his shoulder after an argument because some man does not let stuff go. Not ever even when one is at another prison his life could be in danger. The guy sent a kite. Sometimes it want be an argument it just pop off in the cell.

At this moment me & Tyler can argue , but not get physical. This is what you call being 100 with each other. Just so you now Tyler my celly is 30 years older than me. He from Chicago I never get a person from Tennessee or from Down South. Some guys want cell with another men that is not from the same car. I on the other hand will cell with anybody from any car. As long as the man is straight.

The reason way I am hard I know how to stay in my on space, and I expect the man in my cell to be the same way. Any way else it will be a problem.

This book is not teaching how to live in Terre Haute or any other prison. This book is to show how dangerous prisons are. How unfriendly man can be. How man can be trick out of his life for not being smart. This book was written to stop others from entering into the prison system. Better yet scare you to stay away from a place like Terre Haute or any other prison I want you to see how bad prison is through my eyes, and hope you never make mistakes that will put you in these places.

If I would have got a serious message from a person that really wanted a future for me. The message would have kept me from the wrong people & places.

Please read the words in this book serious. If you are a trouble boy or man. Turn your life in another direction that will only bring out positive outcomes.

Being in so much trouble is not a life to live. If you think being in trouble or causing trouble will bring the girls to you NOT.

Being in trouble gone get your girl taken if you are always in trouble with the law,

Running from them being in and out of prison. All you are doing is giving your girl to another man. The men that are free doing the right thing in the sight of the law he is the one with all the girls . He is always free you are always locked up. Do you get the picture? Stay out and away from trouble.

Stays away from action if it is not gone bring about good outcomes. It is nothing wrong with being bored.

Diamond: When you are bored you thinking. That is how you can come up with a great idea. If you are focus on your thoughts

God will speak to you while you are sitting in the house boring. Because sometimes you need to sit down to get yourself to together and think. Getting a peace of mind is priceless once a man experience so much chaos & confusing.

So sit down and chill in the house instead of running to the streets. Do something productive with your life & time.

While doing something productive with your life in time it will pay off. Someone will notice what you are doing / working hard, and give you a big shot to grow into what you want to be. . A positive altitude will pay off too. To you that are in trouble or about to do something that will cause trouble in your life. Renew your mind into a positive way of thinking.

You will attract what your body is putting out. How you think is what life brings to you. If you are in a positive vibration positive things will come. If you are in a negative vibration negative things will come to you. Stay in a positive vibration people. Connect with positive people.

People like that will motivate you into positive energy. Get around people that will pull out the best out of your life.

Being around great people & energy will change your paradigm in a great way. So stay away from negative places. So you will never have to live in a horrible place like Terre Haute.

I have changed my paradigm in a positive way. Now everything I do go let out a positive vibration and that makes me have no choice but to become someone great in life. The change had to be made. If I wanted to surround myself with uplifting humans. It is nothing better than being around up lifting people. God put me, you on Earth to love one another. Not to steal, kill one another.

This lunch the trays was hot which was pizza, beans, banana. This is one of the trays I like when the tray come in hot. It does not happen often. So every time the food is hot I am thankful I know it is not that serious, but if you are in a cell 24/7 and hungry like I am it is man.

Today I looks out the window looking at the rain while eating. The sun was out at the same time I could not see the sky because it is a metal box covering the top of the window, But it is a spot where I could see the grass Which makes me have to look down. Do you get the picture?

After eating I got back on my exercising routine. The only thing is on my mind at this time was getting out Terre Haute in great shape I was going hard on myself so my set are 100 set ups which I break down in 20 a set. Then 100 2 pump burpees which I do 20 a set, and 500 push-ups which I break down to doing 50 a set.

The thing about my sets I do not rush to finish. The reason being I do all three exercises as one set. After the sets I get a rest by reading my book. It do not take me long to finish my exercising.

In a few hours I am finish doing my exercising. The way I exercise the day goes by fast, and dinner time be close I stopped when the trays was exactly at the door. The exact time was 6:00P.M when I would be finish.

Once I sit on my bunk to eat my tray it was good tray lasagna, beans, and a salad. It did not take me long to eat the little slice that I was giving. My cellmate was finish with his tray too. We both walk to the door at the same time to put our tray down.

After dinner I took me an hour in a half shower. Had to do some planning about what I will do once I get out. First I had to let go of my old ways of thinking. It will be hard because I have to unlearn what I have learned in my past. Learn what I need to learn to set myself up for a better career.

While in the shower I said to myself I will never put a foot in a prison again. Never go back to the streets life again. Sitting in the shower thinking I just could not grabs that so much of my life was wasted out in the streets.

Get your life together before you end up in a place like Terre Haute feeling like a waste. Feeling like a hopeless man.

Out of the shower I got back into my book that I had started reading. This book is about Hinduism the God Ganesh who is a human with an elephant head. He goes around the world teaching people lessons about life. For example it was this king that always invites people over for dinner.

Not from the kindness of his heart, but to show off what he possess. One day he invited Ganesh. Well Ganesh had a big appetite he could eat. He ate all the food the king put on his plate. When all the food was gone he then started eating up the king house. Nothing could stop him, but his mother husband. The King calls him to get Ganesh to stop. His step farther talks him into stop eating.

Diamond: It is a lesson in the story, but you have to figure the lesson out for yourself.

Do not take it the wrong way. Jesus is in my heart I believe in him with all my life. All ways and forever. Nothing will change my relationship with my lord and savior.

That is how I pass time in a cell reading books that spark my intellectual powers reading books that spark that part of the mind that you do not know about. Reading will give you great pleasure. Look at it this way books are soldiers. Build you an army of books. Read ,read , and read some more.

Be wise stay away from negative friends & family members that do not have positive vibrations. It is nothing wrong with being the smart one out of the family. Staying in the house and out of the way will help. Do not get discourage. Being in prison will be the hardest days of your life if you make it out. You will meet your match. If you can fight another man can fight harder I have meet my match a few times. It is alright because what do not kill me will make me stronger. When it is time for me to be release I gone be tough enough for anything that I in encounter.

Today Tuesday March 1, 2016 I woke up before breakfast picked up my radio and turn to listen to 100.7 the morning show. The two hosts were arguing again about something. "Chow time" the guard on duty announced to the range before I could really get into the argument the two was having. The guard opens up the slot which he place two trays on the flap.

Two hot trays & a cold tray. This morning we had pancakes, bacon, and oatmeal.

After eating I went straight back to sleep. Eating then going back to sleep make me sleep better in the SHU. Lunch time came and the trays were at the door. Same thing as usual 4 trays was push through the flap. Chicken patties, pinto beans, spaghetti I smash the whole tray down to nothing.

The same thing I went right back to sleep. Woke up a like an hour before dinner.

I did a few hundred pushups. It was not long until I had to stop because dinner was at the door. Well not exactly but coming down the range I could hear the guard loud keys. Dinner was bullshit beef stroganoff, cornbread, and green beans I had to eat or my stomach would have been on empty this night did not want that to happen to my stomach. So I smash the tray like no food was coming tomorrow.

The rest of the night went by smooth did not get into an argument with Tyler over the chess games we played.

The next morning Wednesday, Hump Day is what the radio host call Wednesday. Hump Day is a day that Terre Haute made up. The only time I heard of Hump Day was when I see a commercial with a camel. I have no idea what Hump Day stand for. This morning I stayed up longer than usual listening to the host. To hear if the host was gone describe to the listeners. What Hump Day was.

He never said what it stands for I went back to sleep after the show went off. Which were 10:00A.M .A few minutes later lunch was at the door. Lunch was super early I was still sleepy. So I put my food up to eat later on tonight. I had an old chip bag in the window that I put my food in when I decide to save something after carefully wrapping my food up I went back to sleep.

Because I went to sleep late last night in the bad my cellmate said "way are you going back to sleep?" We usually stay up doing this time of the day. "My nigga I am going to sleep I am sleepy" I said. "Do not be loud!"

After dinner I did some reading until 9:00P.M. The only reason I set my book down Tyler my celly ask me to play chess. The games we played last three hours. We were both sleepy after playing.

Thursday was a day I like staying up until 10:00P.M listening to my morning show. Thursday is throwback day. All the songs are from the late 80s, 90s, and the early 00s. It is cool listening to all old music from back in the day. That I had forgot about. The songs bring back a few memoirs from my childhood.

The songs had me thinking of the time my mother was taking care of me. The times I did not have to pay for my own cloths. The time I did not have to pay bills. Yeah that is where throwback Thursday took me. It was a great feeling back in them days, but they are over with.

Being in prison so long away from my daughters is not a good feeling. So I chase the stuff that brings on a great feeling in my mind, body, soul. Like listening to my shows, exercising, reading I am not sure that that other inmate. Listening to the channels I do. It does not seem like any other does. The radio gives me private time that I miss in the free world. All I want is some peace and quit in my life & environment with no one else around.

That will be great I am almost home .Well not home, but the half-way house. It will be much better being on common ground. Real Testimony I cannot wait until that day when I am walking out of Terre Haute I am sure that these words was said before, but that is how prison is. Especially having an out date or a date coming up it is very exciting. Real Testimony about me the excitement makes me do crazy things. For example I have lost my date two times already. From be excited about going home. It was confusing to me. One minute I want to get home. The other minute I want to make my family miss me more.

Now I will be extremely careful with myself because I will take off on my cellmate. Over a chess game something is telling me to stop playing chess before a fight breakout because I hate losing. He claim he one of the best players in Terre Haute. That really be getting under my skin I feel like I should be kicking his has in chess. The reason is, I was told when I was only 15 years old how to play chess.

My game should be killing everything he does. It seem like I be playing myself. Which I hate that. Every move I make. He makes the same damn move. Anyway I stop playing chess once I found out his copy my move.

Friday March 3 woke up at 5:30A.M to catch my morning show again. Fridays are almost always good. The host was in a great move this morning I took it as a sign that my day will be great. So far my prediction is right.

For breakfast the guys in the kitchen serve French toast sticks. The whole compound like when the kitchen serves French toast. The whole compound is in the cafeteria in the morning. French toast sticks are not a regular item on the menu.

The item supposed to but, the kitchen workers steal the French toast sticks. Then sale in the unit. All the good items like chicken tenders, pastries, and real steak meat. Are taken to the unit for a profit.

When I was on the compound I was one of the men that like to cook. So any one of them items I mention was in the unit I bought. Only from certain prisoners like the once that take pride in what they are stealing. For example one prisoner brings the food back looking sloppy. The food would be falling out the wrap. Another prisoner would have the food neatly tight wrap. He would be the one I buy from.

It is too many germs that spread around in prison. Plus prisoners be caring diseases too. Being very sanitary is important. Because a man could catch something that could have his arm or leg cut off. That is something I do not want to happen. Being serious about my health is important,

Lunch we had cheese burger with to slices of fake bacon. It was turkey bacon. It was something different. Having a different taste every once in a while is great. Mixing the menu up a few times, not bad right?

After lunch I got back on my exercise routine. Exercising is a must do. Keeping my wind up with my body in shape is important. Like I said before a fight can break out at any minute. Do not want to be the weak man in the fight. Have to always be on guard even though we get alone. Plus I get mad fast I will strike at a millisecond. So I have be in top of the line shape. My opponent will not when against me, and if I do not win it will be a hard fight. That is how prison got a man thinking every day getting out of bed.

Again if you stay in trouble get yourself together. Work on your attitude. Stop using the N word. Use brother in stand. Would you want a Caucasian man to call you the N word? No, so stop using that word.

Stay away from drug infests places. It is more ways to make money than selling drugs. All you have to do is sit down and think of something. Invent something that does not exist in the world.

Stop wasting your time around people that really do not care about your future. If the person does not love his or her self, what make you think he or she will love you? Start really loving yourself because if you love yourself. The vibration you are in will attract another person that loves their self.

First you got to love and care for yourself before you can show that type of feeling toward another person. Stop doing drugs too that has an effect on your mind, body and soul the stuff is poison. Cleanse yourself from the man made poison that is meant to destroy what God made It will make you stronger and alert in life.

Get away from them negative places because if you stay in the place you are in. The only place for you is prison or dead. Then if you are lucky enough to end up in prison. You will still feel like you are dead. Then reality gone strike if you are smart. You will notice that the streets are not worth living in. Being so negative is not the way to live. So again read this book carefully.

Get something out of my life experience It is a real testimony t . And turn your life around. Chase, strive after something positive it will eventually pay off.

It is time for you to change for the better. If you are reading this book. God is talking to you through the testimonies in this book man. personally never had to use it. Every time I had a problem in a cell. It always got physical. Exercise keep me a step ahead. Because behind these doors a man got to be in shape. It is survival of the fittest in prison.

Saturday lunch was serve at 1:30P.M which is late. The guys on the range was pissed I could hear other inmates on the door. Arguing with the guard while he was passing out the trays. My cellmate said" Them trays better be hot." really I could not get into all that I did not care if the food had ice in it at this point. My time is almost up I do not want the guards to say I had something to do with a riot. If one pop off over the trays being cold. One more write I will be stuck in the SHU into June.

A frivolous shot will break my heart at this point. Just thinking about the last time my date was lost. Make me sick to my stomach. Lunch came to the door I put it up for later tonight.

On this Saturday I did not exercise it was a rest day. Not exercising make the weekend move by slow, but I got a few more books to read. Always having a few books on hand is a fetish of mine. Reading books is powerful reading help build a person vocabulary. Reading also keep my mind from being trap behind these doors.

Other guys read books. Not the books that will help sharping ones life the right way I stay away from them type of books . Every book I hear them guys yell & trade on the range. The book is either a murder mystery or hood book. My type of books got to be uplifting, knowledgeable, healthy.

Getting that positive attitude out of people is the way of life for me now. Do something good for myself and something good for someone else each day. It will be a action or a positive. Word.

A few hours of reading is great for my brain muscle. The reason I keep hitting hard about reading books I will love if you put your mind in reading a good book like Successful Intelligence. Plus I want you to change the way you are living I mean this from the heart. If you . Think about the picture I have painted for you. Who in their right mind will still do the things that will put them in prison if one is caught. A dumb person that is who.

May 9th exactly eight days until I walk out Terre Haute. The lip boxing started early this morning on the range. For some reason this Miami cat keep going against the car. He got me thinking he with the gay squad. For the past five days I been fighting on the door. The only reason I jump off my bed and run to the door. Is because I heard my name in somebody mouth on the range. Every time this happen I tell myself I will not get on the door anymore I know how I am once I feel played.

May 10 seven days left. This morning I woke up around 5:00A.M to pray. It felt good to. Knowing God then got me through all this time. A week left and I will be walking out of Terre Haute. On my way to the half- way house in Nashville common ground. And the best thing is no one knows I am on my way home.

Last meals At Terre Haute Breakfast yellow grits, chocolate cupcake, and green Cantaloupe. Lunch- Chicken patty, rice, and beans. With cookies for dessert. Dinner –meat loaf, mashed potatoes,corn, and beans. Plus I had a milk from this morning.

May 11 this morning woke up at 6:00A.M I turned on my radio to 100.7. The host was speaking on Hump Day. Only people in Terre Haute know what he is talking about I been listening to him for a while know, and I still do not know what Hump Day stand for.

Breakfast –pancakes ,cinnamon oatmeal, and a apple I stayed up until until walk through left. Walk through is when all the top staff come on the range. Every inmate be at there door. To talk to the warden about a problem. Or there unit team. Lunch we had cheeseburgers, fries, and red beans and

156

rice. Two cookies for dessert. Dinner soft tacos, 2 kind of beans , which one set of beans was from lunch, and rice with chopped up hamburger meat that was from lunch too. After eating all my food I was really full.

May 12 five more days two to freedom. On this morning I woke up at 6:00A.M to listen to the radio again, which was throwback Thursday. As I am listening he plays a song I have not heard in a long time Fresh Prince Girls Aren't Nothing but trouble. Lunch – Fish, bean, and pasta. Plus a ice cream bar. Dinner we had tune salad, beans from the lunch tray, and beans.

May 13 four more days left I woke up still sleepy from staying up late last night. I and Tyler had a conversation about outer space. This morning breakfast was French toast, oatmeal, and one banana I went back to sleep until lunch. The tray had a chicken which was hot this time around, beans, and sweet potatoes. Dinner – chicken fried rice, beans ,and carrots mix with broccoli. Carrots with broccoli mix get the picture in your head. It will make you sick to your stomach like it did me when I ate it. If you never want to eat a meal like this. Stay away from bad places & people. Change the way you are living for a better life. It will take time to change the bad habits, but they have to change if you want stuff to work in your favor. Make sure you make adjustments in your life as soon as you finish reading this book. So you will not become another statistic living in a cell.

May 14 three days left until I am free. Breakfast –brown corn flakes a donut , and one banana. Lunch two hot dogs, tater tots , and that was lunch. Around 6:00A.M dinner was at the door spaghetti, beans, and bread. When I went to sleep this night my stomach was on empty. Not a good feeling.

May 15 two days left breakfast we had brown flakes one donut again. Even if I got two days left I really am sick of brown flakes, but I got to eat so my body will function right. It was Sunday I had to get my radio and tone in to Ryan Seacrest. Meghan Trainer was hosting the show. She made me feel better. Brunch was at the door so I had to get up to get my tray. . Pancakes, eggs and a slice of ham with a piece of green Cantaloupe I had my milk saved from my breakfast tray. Dinner was some type of chili mac that I have never seen green beans and red beans with rice.

May 16 a wake up left. In other words tomorrow I will be walking out of Terre Haute... This morning for breakfast biscuit with gravy, oatmeal and a banana. Lunch we was serve chicken wraps, salad, and potatoes that look gray. This was a horrible lunch. Dinner –Pork, bake potato with sour cream. With a salad too which I did not eat.

May 17 I woke up ready to go I was thinking a guard would come and get me before any one on the range will know. Wrong that thought was thought out wrong. After hours went pass I was still in a cell. At this point every guard that walked down the range I was asking. What is up with me being release? Man I was getting mad at how the guards was treating my question. The guards that I asked did not come back with the answer. All I was thinking is something then went left. Not a good feeling at all.

Finally a lieutenant walked to my cell and said "Buckner pack your things. You are leaving. "Man that is an understatement I was already pack I been packed for hours.

Well anyway I was handcuffed then escorted to the front desk. The same place where I was booked in. Now I was getting process out of Terre Haute. The guard hands me all the property I had in the storage. As you now I have not seen these items in months. One pair of my shoes was covered in mold. They went in the trash.

The only items I pack to take with me were my Federal paperwork. A couple books that I enjoyed reading. This was The Sam Walton, "Light up your Child Mind". The rest of the items I just left in the holding cell.

It was a few grand that I had on my account that I was ready to count I have not had money in my hand in years. So I was ready for Terre Haute to give me my cash. But it was not given to me in cash. My few grand was on a debit card. It was alright with me as long as every dollar was on it.

After getting my money I was still not yet free. Now I had to wait on a cab driver to pull up. He was to drop me off at the bus station. It was another 15 minute wait before he walks through the door. He was a Mexican man that I did not take as my cab driver because he was not dress in cab cloths. He walks up to me to let me know he was my ride to freedom. Yes I was finally free. To be continued.

Diamond: to the reader

If you do not have your High school diploma or GED make getting an education a priority in your life. Having some form of education will open up doors you thought could not be open. It did for me it can for you. Sincerely, Bruce Buckner

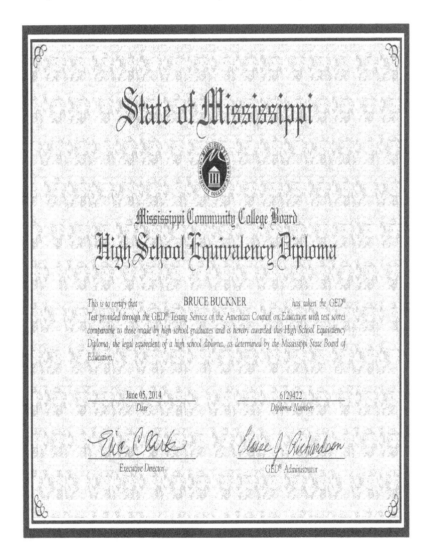

CERTIFICATE OF

COMPLETION

Bruce Buckner

11/2/2015

Has successfully met all of the requirements

for completion of the

"V.T. Computer Applications"

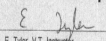

E. Tyler, V.T. Instructor

CERTIFICATE OF

COMPLETION

Bruce Buckner

11-2-2015

Has successfully met all of the requirements

for completion of the

"Keyboarding"

E. Tyler, V.T. Instructor

Brightwood College

Nashville Campus

Perfect Attendance Certificate

In honor of achieving perfect attendance in the
Medical Billing and Coding program,
Brightwood College proudly acknowledges

Bruce Buckner

For perfect attendance achievement
during the October term.

_____
Campus President

Brightwood College

Nashville Campus

Perfect Attendance Certificate

In honor of achieving perfect attendance in the
Medical Billing and Coding program,
Brightwood College proudly acknowledges

Bruce Buckner

For perfect attendance achievement
during the September 2016 term.

_____
Campus President

SI SPANN INSURANCE, INC.

Insurance, Bonds & Financial Services
Since 1951

710 Thompson Lane, P.O. Box 40366, Nashville, TN 37204
Telephone: (615) 383-8000   Facsimile: (615) 383-8926
National: (800) 932-5638   National: (800) 329-2663

NOTARY PUBLIC BOND -- STATE OF TENNESSEE

STATE OF TENNESSEE
COUNTY OF DAVIDSON   BOND NUMBER: 16-11/03

Know All Men By These Presents That We,

Bruce Quentin Buckner Jr
676 Putnam Dr
Nashville, TN 37218

As Principal, and the Contractors Bonding and Insurance Company, an Illinois insurance corporation duly licensed to do business in the State of Tennessee, as Surety, acknowledge ourselves firmly bound unto the State of Tennessee, in the sum of TEN THOUSAND & No/100 DOLLARS ($10,000.00), for the payment of which, well and truly to be made, we bind ourselves and our legal representatives, jointly and severally by these presents.

The condition of this bond is such, that if the named principal, who has been elected NOTARY PUBLIC in the STATE OF TENNESSEE, shall faithfully perform the duties of the office of Notary Public, then this obligation shall become null and void, otherwise it shall remain in full force and effect.

Effective Date of Bond: 11/03/16
Expiration Date of Bond: 11/03/20

Important: *Must Be Signed In The County Clerk's Office*

PLEASE SIGN HERE: ....
                        NOTARY PUBLIC - As Approved

Contractors Bonding and Insurance Company

by: ....
        TN Agent & Attorney-In-Fact
        SPANN INSURANCE, INC.

YOU **MUST** TAKE this bond to County Clerk Brenda Wynn's office and sign the Oath of Office to receive your Notary Commission which will then allow you to notarize documents.

AN ERROR & OMISSIONS POLICY WAS **NOT** PURCHASED IN CONJUNCTION WITH THIS BOND.

Our family business appreciates insuring your family and business!

THE STATE OF TENNESSEE

To All Who Shall See These Presents ... Greetings:
Know Ye, That, whereas the Legislative Body of Davidson County
at its October 2016 meeting appointed

BRUCE QUENTIN BUCKNER JR
State of Tennessee Notary Public

Now Therefore, I, Bill Haslam, Governor of the State of Tennessee, do hereby certify that said BRUCE QUENTIN BUCKNER JR
a Notary Public for the State of Tennessee is authorized to act in any County in the State of Tennessee
until the expiration of the term on Tuesday, November 3, 2020.

In Witness Whereof, I, Bill Haslam, Governor and Tre Hargett, Secretary of State, hereto,
affixed our hand and the Great Seal of the State in Nashville on Thursday, November 3, 2016.

Bill Haslam, Governor

Tre Hargett, Secretary of State

CERTIFICATE OF APPRECIATION

DAVIDSON COUNTY JUVENILE DETENTION CENTER-MOTIVATIONAL SPEAKER

Bruce Buckner

		12/28/17
YOLANDA HOCKETT	ASST. DIRECTOR OF PROGRAMS	DATE

HTC

HIGH TICKET CLOSER

CERTIFICATE
OF ACHIEVEMENT

BRUCE BUCKNER

PRESENTED THIS
4TH DAY OF JANUARY 2018
FOR SUCCESSFUL COMPLETION OF
THE HIGH TICKET CLOSER™
CERTIFICATION PROGRAM

DAN LOK, KING OF HIGH TICKET SALES™

KAYVON, ONE CALL CLOSER™

ADMISSION CERTIFICATE

DAYMOND JOHN'S SUCCESS FORMULA TEAM PRESENTS

3-DAY WORKSHOP

Friday - Sunday
February 23, 24, and 25, 2018

Millennium Maxwell House Nashville
2025 Rosa L. Parks Boulevard
Nashville, TN 37228

Registration for the workshop will be at **8:30** in the morning.
The **workshop** will start each morning at **9:00 am**.

Congratulations!
Success starts here.

"TRIPLE YOUR INVESTMENT"
GUARANTEE CERTIFICATE

Daymond John's Success Formula Team (the "Company") knows time is important to fully implement the techniques, strategies and training you will learn at the Workshop. The Company guarantees that if you take the actions taught by the Daymond John's Success Formula team and fully implement the training you receive by running twenty-five (25) advertising/marketing campaigns for your product, service or idea and do not receive a minimum of **THREE TIMES** your investment in sales, we will **give your money back**. This guarantee is subject to the following conditions:

1. You must attend all of the Workshop. During the following six (6) months, you must run at least 25 advertising/marketing campaigns for your product, service or idea using the techniques taught at the Workshop. There is no minimum budget requirement for the campaigns.

2. If, after six (6) months, you have not had sales of at least THREE TIMES your tuition, the Company will refund your investment.

3. Documentation of the steps you have taken to implement the campaigns (advertising invoice copies, etc.) must be received by the Company before the end of the sixth calendar month following your purchase. Documentation must be sent by U.S. Mail or courier to the following address: Success Formula LLC, 1810 E Sahara Ave. #100 Las Vegas, NV 89104.

4. You must also provide proof of purchase of the Workshop (such as a copy of your Purchase Order) AND a copy of this certificate.

5. This guarantee does not apply to any further educational service which you may purchase in the future.

Tuition reimbursement requests are reviewed on a case-by-case basis which may take up to sixty (60) calendar days.

Bruce Buckner

Student Name   Date Authorized

REV012417 – ZSFTICERT

CPSIA information can be obtained
at www.ICGtesting.com
Printed in the USA
LVHW081326160619
621372LV00012B/389/P

9 780578 202495